NO
GROWN-UPS
IN HEAVEN

NO GROWN-UPS IN HEAVEN

A T-A PRIMER FOR CHRISTIANS
(and others)

Art Greer

HAWTHORN BOOKS, INC.
W. Clement Stone, Publisher
New York

Transactional Analysis
Psychology, Religious

NO GROWN-UPS IN HEAVEN

Library of Congress Catalog Card Number: 74-33595

ISBN: 0-8015-5404-7

1 2 3 4 5 6 7 8 9 10

To Barbara . . .

To Danny . . .

To Julie . . .

The Kids I'm growing with!

Contents

Acknowledgments

Numerous saints have contributed to my understanding of both the gospel and transactional analysis. If I remember an individual's contribution, I will credit him. In many cases I will not remember.

I give broad credit to Eric Berne (the founder of TA), Tom and Amy Harris, Muriel James, Dorothy Jongeward, Claude Steiner, Jack Dusay, Frank Ernst, Steve Karpman, and especially Anita Plummer and Bob and Mary Goulding, who showed me what to do with the knowledge. I also particularly thank the Rev. Phil Gruenke of MacPherson, Kansas. Phil's incredibly beautiful Child hooked mine on the whole idea of TA. He coined the term "mustoughtshoulds" ("muss-TAUT-shoods") and described the "on/off switches" and "volume controls" in ego states.

I am indebted to all the Bible writers and to theologians, seminary people, pastors and lay persons of many parishes, and colleagues who have helped me with my faith.

When I think an idea is uniquely mine, I'll say so. Otherwise, I don't take credit for the concepts, only the particular pot this batch is stewing in—a unique, natural child of God . . . ME!

NO
GROWN-UPS
IN HEAVEN

1
A New Way to Go

Hundreds of times I had read St. Paul's proclamation describing how he and all the brethren groaned, longed, and sighed with anxiety for immortality (2 Corinthians 5:2-4). I'd read it with a grain of salt, because I heard a lot of folk talking about how they could hardly wait to get to heaven, but nobody seemed in a terrible hurry to arrange passage. In any event, I couldn't use what St. Paul said, nor could my Christian friends. I assumed his words were just another example of what I *should* be like if only I were worth the powder to blow me to hell, which I apparently wasn't. Someday I would try harder and maybe I would get there.

Then one day I stumbled on this same passage in the New English Bible. (Stumbling isn't *all* bad.) Reading the crystal-clear English of today's people, I understood what St. Paul had wanted me to hear: He was perfectly willing to assume the tent of immortality so long as he didn't have to give up anything he already had—namely, this earthly life. That was something I could identify with!

For the first time I understood this passage. The reason: Someone had said it in such a way that The Little Boy Inside Me could figure it out and accept it. All the earlier translations were written, it seemed, for my great-grandparents, not me.

Most of us really don't want to go to heaven. As many visualize it, heaven sounds about as exciting as "Happy Hour" at an old folks' home. The idea of spending eternity with stuffy, pious grown-ups, sitting on horsehair sofas fanning themselves with funeral-home fans while the sweat trickles down over their bat-winged collars, is simply too much for us five-year-olds to endure. Even a fresh batch of pictures for the stereopticon would not rescue heaven from resembling a long, hot Sunday afternoon with Aunt Cunnigunda.

Honestly, can you get excited at the thought of our spending eternity quoting cliche scriptures to one another? Phooey! This book is offered in case you haven't heard the good news: Heaven will be at least as neat a place as earth is, because . . .

There are no grown-ups in heaven—just children! "Truly, I say to you, whoever does not receive the kingdom of God like a child shall not enter it!" (Matthew 18:3).

I will be describing the Child ego state in detail in Chapter 5. For now I'll just say that the Child—or Kid, as I sometimes call him—is that part of us that experiences life pretty much as we did at age five or six. It's what we experience and feel when we laugh or cry, are brave or scared, have fun or are solemn.

I believe all therapy (change) takes place when one person's Child convinces another person's Child that there is a neater way to live. I also believe all education (as opposed to training) and all preaching (as opposed to religious lecturing) take place Child-to-Child. I think people seldom really *learn* anything that's useful for themselves unless they're having fun doing it. They may dutifully store information for a rainy day, but they won't use it right then while basking in the sunshine.

I want you to learn some instantly useful stuff and have some fun, too, as you read this. I plan to have fun while I write it. As you read, you are welcome to laugh, giggle, roll on the floor, or whatever it is you do when having a good time. This book is written primarily by my Child to the Child inside you. I'm aware you are an "intelligent" person with a complete "value system." There are textbookish books on TA for that part of you. I am writing to the Little Boy or Little Girl who says, "I don't know what's right or wrong, true or false, but I sure do know what I like and need and want and feel!" (Kids listen good when other Kids talk, especially when it's about something that Kids want to hear. Most of all, Kids want to know how to make it in their neighborhood.)

This book is about two things my Kid has found important in the neighborhood of life, the Christian gospel and transactional analysis. These tools—the one Jesus gave us and the one Eric Berne and others have given us—can be used to change your life.

I want to share with you my image of the person I'm writing for. My imaginary reader has been "up and down the road" a time or two; is intelligent and aware; is not always happy about how his life is going, yet is doing moderately well by the usual standards. She senses something is missing but isn't sure what. Somewhere along the line he has been involved with the church, maybe still is. She finds real value in her religious searchings, yet is having trouble "getting with" all the concepts and doctrines. He wonders why he isn't enjoying life more and why his religion isn't more useful. He suspects the church has somehow gotten away from a faith that healed—at least there isn't much healing going on in *his* church. Sometimes she wishes someone would find the time-control dial and turn it back to "start." For all her nostalgia, however, my reader is open to new ideas and new approaches. He is willing to undertake changes in himself when and if the ideas and approaches make sense and seem safe enough.

With this person in mind, I feel comfortable writing the way I lecture and talk. I won't fret about "writing properly" or saying things "the right way." Through years of experience I've found my loose style and loose language communicate well with the person I've described.

I want you to open yourself to hearing and seeing things differently. Moreover, I want you to understand transactional analysis and the message of Jesus not only in your head but also in your stomach. By the time you get to the Postlude, I'd like you to be *feeling* what life can be about.

I recognize that the Christian faith covers a lot of territory that TA isn't interested in, not now anyhow. TA doesn't purport to be involved with moral or ethical issues and concerns such as the purpose of life, values, or direction—although many TA leaders are. I am not equating TA with the gospel. I'm not saying TA is the Savior. I'm not suggesting that Jesus was a transactional analyst unawares. (If Jesus ever used a couch, he didn't make a big deal of it.) I do think that insofar as TA overlaps the gospel, it agrees with and amplifies many of Jesus' instructions about how we can become the authentic persons we were created to be.

My purpose in this book is twofold: to create an interesting gut-level understanding of introductory TA theory and application; and to invite you to take a second look at the gospel. Some of those people on the radio and in the pulpit have been distorting what The Man said.

Transactional analysis is more than a gimmick, although God knows there are enough people trying to gimmick it to death these days. I see TA as a gift from God, intended to free people from the chains that imprison them. The church has called these chains "sin"—a word often used by bossy people to grind other people into the ground. I've used TA and the gospel in combination to help people shed the chains that bind and blind. The mixture works.

If you find something good in these pages, use it to work on the mote in your own eye. Later you can help your friends with their private splinters—if they ask you to. But like prayer, TA isn't to be tinkered with. It really works, so expect your life to be changed if you apply it seriously.

But NOTE—TA is more than just a "language." It is a way of seeing life and exploring ourselves and others. Like the gospel, TA doesn't become useful just because we learned some new words. We're about a new way of life, not a new vocabulary, and *that* comes with a lot of practice in using the concepts in our daily life.

When lives change for the better, I see the Lord at work. This kind of change *is* possible. I invite you to see for yourself.

2

Such a Crowd in My Head

If you were a Martian dropping in on us from outer space, you wouldn't operate on the basis of assumptions the way you do now. You'd always ask, "What's going on now?"

To you, an Earth Person, a room full of people with their heads bowed suggests prayer. (Unless they're moving around and have their eyes open, in which case you'd figure they're hunting for someone's contact lens.) But a Martian wouldn't have a background that would say "prayer." He wouldn't recite the Lord's Prayer without first receiving an explanation of what it's all about. This book is a manual for thinking and talking "Martian." The analogy was drawn by Eric Berne, who saw transactional analysis as a whole new way of looking at ourselves, others, and our relationships.

It's fun to learn Martian. It leads us to ask odd questions, with surprising results. Consider, for example, an experience of one of my trainees, a Methodist pastor with a long history of "trying to help people." One morning a member of his flock proceeded to dump half a dozen problems in his lap: "My husband's leaving me; my son has contracted syphilis; my daughter has flunked out of school . . . and just a while ago the cake I was baking fell."

Therapists call people like this "throw-up artists."

Sickened by the soured emotional mess inside them, they find a "helper" who will let them use his lap as a dumping place. Since most helpers are accustomed to Earth-think, they automatically assume that the other person wants to be helped. After all, this lady wouldn't have come all the way over to the church if she didn't want to be helped, would she? Besides, the helper feels compelled to help someone—it's essential to his sense of vocation.

But this helper was different. He learned some Martian. He pushed aside his personal need to be a handy-dandy expert and he swallowed the pat, 1-2-3-4 advice that sat on the tip of his tongue. Instead, he gently but firmly asked the lady a Martian question, "What would you like for me to do about all this?"

"I—I guess I want you to give me your opinions about my problems," she said.

This brought another Martian question, "And if I gave you my opinions, what would you do with them?"

This really threw her. For two full minutes she sat and puzzled over his last question and her feelings about it.

"I wouldn't do anything," she said.

Although she was surprised to hear herself saying this, she somehow felt relieved, and settled back in her chair.

"So, what do you want me to hear?" asked the Martian pastor.

"I want you to know what a pile of bad luck has come my way," she said.

In three brief transactions the pastor had cut through the Rackets and Games that the lady and her past helpers had engaged in. Now she recognized that she didn't want a batch of "solutions," but some attention and support.

"In my pre-TA days," he said to me later, "I would have spent months trying to 'solve' this woman's problems. I would have failed, because she would have received my attention in such a crooked, roundabout way. We would have wound up feeling angry with each other. TA helped us cut through the veneer and subterfuge, and we were open and honest with ourselves and with each other."

It all began in San Francisco in Eric Berne's treatment room. A conventional psychoanalyst, he used the theories of Sigmund Freud to help people work their way through their "head problems." One day, as I understand the story, he was working with a middle-aged man who reported he had a little boy trapped inside him. No doubt there was a standard response to such a statement (something about sex, I suppose), but for some reason Berne shunned it. What if, he wondered, his patient really *had* a little boy inside him? Even more intriguing, what if the little guy talked? At that time, no self-respecting analyst believed either to be possible.

Berne told his patient he wanted to talk to the little boy for a while. The man complied, and as he talked, Eric noticed changes. The patient's voice took a higher pitch; his body language became that of a little fellow; his vocabulary shrank, and his concepts became simpler. Eric was talking to a five-year-old!

Once we become aware of a new phenomenon, we tend to recognize it wherever it's to be found. Remember when you decided to marry and began to think about furnishing your home? I do. I walked into a dime store with Barbara and was amazed to discover they sold pots and pans and potato peelers! Berne's experience was like that. After that first patient he could spot a little boy or little girl in each of his patients. With time and practice he learned how to get through to the little guy. And he could distinguish which was talking, the adult or the five-year-old.

This was back in the early 1950s. He shared his findings with some fellow psychiatrists, and they began gathering in his home once a week to discuss this idea and how it was working in their practices. This group later became the San Francisco Transactional Analysis Seminar, and from it grew the International TA Association, which certifies and trains transactional analysts.

The therapists reported occasional difficulties in talking to the Adult. The Child was fairly clear, but not so the Adult. (In TA we capitalize these words when speaking of ego states in order to differentiate them from the biological parent or the offspring child.)

Some of you older readers will remember a movie *The Three Faces of Eve,* and younger people may have seen it on TV. This pre-TA movie explored a new phenomenon being encountered by therapists: Eve had three totally different personalities, each of them unaware of the other two. TA practitioners wouldn't find this case all that novel. They would see each of Eve's "personalities" as an extension of one of her ego states.

Casual readers of TA frequently assume that when we speak of "ego states" we're just fiddling around with Freud's "Ego, Superego, and Id." Not so. He lumped human behavior and processes into three useful but rather abstract piles. He spoke of the Id, which only roughly corresponds to the Child ego state, as a seething cauldron of chaotic forces. The Unconscious was almost unreachable and unpredictable, and it could erupt at any moment to destroy an otherwise calm life.

Eric Berne's "ego state," on the other hand, describes a highly organized collection of ways to behave, to think, to feel. It operates consistently and is extremely predictable in any given situation. Today my Child giggles pretty much as he did years ago and at the same kinds of things (like pompous folk falling on their duffs). Today my Parent can get as irritated at horseplay as he did when a schoolmate put chewing gum on my pencil eraser. Ego states have to do with real people with real names and addresses and phone numbers. They aren't hazy concepts. One of Berne's main contributions was to show us that we can quite predictably spot an ego state in ourselves and in others once we have mastered the "Martian" skills.

Three people! Our heads are pretty crowded. Recall the complicated conversations you sometimes have with yourself driving down the freeway? Lots of diverse opinions; so many arguments go on in there. As the father in *Fiddler on the Roof* kept saying, "But on the other hand . . ."

Jesus said, "A kingdom divided against itself is laid waste (Mark 3:24)," and that's precisely what happens when people "have their heads messed up." The equipment itself isn't bad; the trouble is that the equipment is working against its owner instead of for him!

Before we can begin to achieve consensus among this crowd inside our head, we must get acquainted with them, and we'll begin in the next chapter.

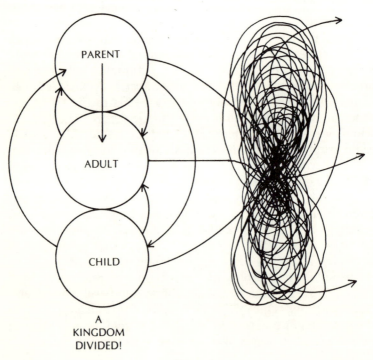

PARENT

ADULT

CHILD

A
KINGDOM
DIVIDED!

Figure 1

3

What Am I Supposed to Be Like?

It's a big lie about how happy everyone's childhood was. You had a tough row to hoe. One of your very first problems upon emerging into the world was a tough one—figuring out what you were supposed to be like.

Researchers took newborn monkeys and isolated them from all other monkeys. They hand-fed them and the like. Without the presence of older monkeys, the young ones had no way of knowing what a monkey was supposed to be like. Thus, when they were grown, they didn't act like monkeys. Folklore is full of stories about cats that were raised with dogs and ended up barking.

But you weren't isolated. During your first five or six years you took in approximately 25,000 hours of information describing what it meant to be a "grown-up" in your family. This input was stored in your head on what we call "Parent tapes." You absorbed this information in a rather uncritical fashion because your evaluating equipment wasn't very keen. You heard it—and in it went!

Most of these data came from your parents (or whoever raised you), and more from mom than from dad, likely, because she spent more time with you. These were the "big guns," but they were helped by aunts and uncles and grandparents and older brothers and sisters. As you stared wide-eyed around you, you absorbed a lot of "facts." "Niggers are shiftless," daddy always said, and before you understood what that meant, *click, click, click,* you put it on a Parent tape. It was a "true" statement because daddy wouldn't have said it unless it was true, right? That's what a little no-necked kid surrounded by giants has to conclude. They wouldn't lie, would they? Besides, you didn't really understand what "lie" meant.

Mom always said, "Life is a terrible sad vale of tears." *Click, click, click,* straight into your head. There were 25,000 hours of that kind of thing. "Children are to be seen and not heard." "The best people in life are Congregationalists." "People are always out to get you." "A woman's place is in the home." *Click, click, click.*

TA calls this particular collection *Parent* tapes because they compose the Parent ego state. We have a diagram that is standard for showing ego states:

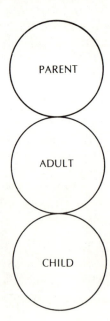

Figure 2

That top circle represents the Parent, a highly organized collection of data—your "program" of what grown-ups were supposed to be like. The info came in assorted ways, but usually through the words of the grown-ups around you and in the form of orders, advice, slogans, truisms, morals, "truths," and values. You stored information about how you were supposed to act and feel in certain situations. "When people insult you, you're supposed to get mad; everyone does." "When people come into a room, smile at them to show them you're friendly." "Keep your legs crossed." "Nice girls don't slouch." "Big boys don't cry." "No one in our family is ever successful." "Don't look too happy or the Evil Eye will get you." "If you have a dirty thought, God will punish you."

You also stored data about how to sit when pondering a serious question, how to listen in an "interested" way, and how to alter your voice in different situations. Have you ever caught yourself sitting or standing or gesturing in a particular way and remarked to yourself, "Wow, that's exactly the way dad used to sit"?

When I am "in my Parent" (ego state), I act, think, feel, and respond as someone before me did; that is, I do all this in a learned fashion. This is the way I am supposed to act (or feel or think).

Remember, I said you stored all this information in an uncritical (not-looked-at) way. When I am in my Parent, I am always right. "No, dammit, I am not being opinionated! Women really *are* weaker than men." (That's what daddy always said, and he wouldn't have said it unless it was true.) You can see, then, that the Parent has absolutely no reasoning power. Why should it reason when it already has all the "facts"? Consequently, the Parent usually has a terrible case of the "mustoughtshoulds." It knows precisely what you (and everyone else) *must* do, *ought* to do, and *should* do. Listen to two Parents talking about politics. They have utter clarity! If they're in agreement, it isn't too bad, just boring. But if they disagree, wow! Since they're both "right," the argument has no place to go. They're locked in mortal combat.

Before we get too far into this, a note of warning. It's fashionable among TA neophytes to "Parent spot." When they spot someone's Parent, they beat him over the head with it. Don't assume that the Parent is always bad. My Parent is useful to me a lot of the time. Mom and Dad put a lot of good stuff in my head that still serves me well.

Current critics of TA complain that we "put down the Parent" and allow folk to blame their mom and dad for their problems.* Not so! The development of a healthy Parent ego state (that is, a set of moral values that work and a way to nurture ourselves and others) is *critically* important.

The important issue here is that the Parent tapes that cause us problems are almost invariably those that we were forced to incorporate and that *no longer* (if they ever did) *make sense.*

Since these recordings were etched in acid on tungsten steel tapes by the time I was six or so, they are *old*! Most of *my* Parent tapes were in place by 1934. That makes them archaic. (Dr. Harry Boyd says we too often insist upon "having archaic and eating it too."**) Because Parent tapes are dated, they need to be checked for their current usefulness. Tapes that once were useful may or may not be useful to me now. Some may not have been valid in the first place. So I must continually review my library of Parent tapes.

Let's look at one of my Parent tapes, "You shouldn't take off your pants in mixed company." This tape has been useful. You can't imagine how many jails it has kept me out of. Usually it computes. But what if, as I begin to lecture, I stick my pipe in my pocket and it sets my pants on fire. My Parent tape would not be useful here; indeed, if I decide to accept it as God's absolute truth, it may be my *last* decision.

My Parent keeps me out of illegal parking spots, gets me out of the sack in the morning, and keeps me eating three

---

*See Thomas C. Oden, *Game Free* (New York: Harper & Row, 1974), pp. 87 ff. Oden is a responsible scholar. I wish he had checked with more analysts on the importance of Parent tapes.

**Harry Boyd, Ph.D., is a Teaching Member of ITAA in Oklahoma City. Besides being a potent therapist and trainer, he is *funny.*

square meals a day. (In contrast, my Adult merely observes the consequences of not eating, while my Child wants to eat when he's hungry, and damn the hour.) Thus the Parent may be good, may be bad, may be indifferent. May be inaccurate, may be helpful, may be terribly harmful (especially when the Parent is crazy, as when the person's Parent keeps telling him to kill himself).

An effective way to study the Parent ego state is to break it down into two components: the Nurturing Parent and the Critical Parent.

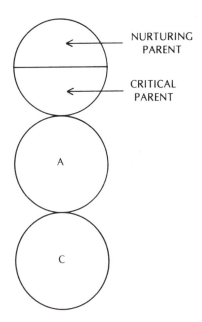

Figure 3

First, the Nurturing Parent. As I looked at big people during my first five or so years, I observed that they had a way of taking care of one another—nurturing one another. As I absorbed information on how to care for other people (and myself), I filed it in the Nurturing Parent compartment of my head. What I know about "knowing how" to nurture depends, of course, upon the nurturing character of my model.

My chief model was my mother, who had a real case of what Eric Berne called "the Jewish Mother Syndrome." She was never without her Hot Bowl of Chicken Soup to make things well. She nurtured me to pieces.

As a child I had a tendency to be "sickly"—a tendency that I cultivated once I found out how much nurture it could evoke. I could produce a "sickly" in five minutes' time. I had upwards of twenty "colds" a season. On occasion one of my colds had its *own* cold. In my prime I could have four different colds going at the same time. With mom's Parent cheering me on I became expert at susceptibility. On an autumn evening I would walk out on the porch and she would yell, "Get out of that Night Air. Do you want to catch a cold?" I wanted to! And I would come back into the house and begin to manufacture one.

As soon as I produced my first sniffle, mom would hand out the 4-Way Cold Tablets, which were a kind of prehistoric antihistamine. She also plied me with hot toddies complete with a touch of rock 'n' rye. She would fluff up the pillows, get me into bed, bring my books, and write excuses to the teachers. Every five minutes her Nurturing Parent would check to make sure I was comfy. I acknowledge that being kept in bed *after* school hours wasn't much fun, and neither was having to swallow some of that vile stuff, but I sure did eat up the nurture! "You have to invest something to get something," dad always said.

I came out of seminary sniffling and snorting—and sporting a new wife. Barbara's mother, a registered nurse, nurtured a sick person by getting out of his way so he would have room to get well in. ("How can they get well with you hovering over them?") It follows that Barb had some definite ideas about how one person was supposed to care for another person. And since the ideas were in her Parent, they were the *right* way!

Now the stage is set for either some old-fashioned conflict—or change.

One morning I decided I needed some extra Nurture Strokes. (This kind of thinking always takes place in the bowels rather than in the brain. It's preconscious—we don't consciously decide.) I woke up with all the bodily signs that I was set to do a "bad cold." Maybe some Night Air had seeped through the windows, or maybe I had on one blanket too many. "Too many blankets can cause colds," mother always said.

In my getting-ready-to-die, feeble-male-in-great-pain voice, I said, "Barb, call the chapel and have them prepare my memorial service. I'm not going to make it."

"I'll do that," she said cheerily, and left the room, shutting the door behind her. I sank into my pillow of pain and began waiting for my Hot Chicken Soup. Meanwhile I went into my usual feverish coma. (Nurturing Parents don't give the ultimate in service unless you convince them it's worth their while.) When I came to again, my watch told me it was 6:30 P.M. That damned door had not opened *once* since 8:30 A.M. "You stuff a cold and starve a fever," mother always said. I wasn't going through all that trouble just to starve, and I was starving.

Barbara had been busily nurturing me, but as *she* knew nurture to be. It wasn't a matter of who's right, although if you ever need to pick a fight, this is a handy issue. It was simply a matter of how each of us had learned to be "helpful" to others and how we thought others should help us. Barb understood that if I needed her enough, I would scream for her; meanwhile she went about her tasks.

(That day, twenty years ago, must have been traumatic. I don't remember *deciding* anything, but I haven't "done a cold" very many times since. And I don't think I've avoided Night Air all that much. We just don't reward "sicklies" at our house!)

Your Nurturing Parent not only ' 'knows how" to care for

people but is also tender, concerned, sentimental, loving. It's the Nurturing Parent who likes to sit and look through old college yearbooks and find joy remembering how nice it was back in the good old days "when things were right." He likes to ask questions like "Are you comfortable?" "Can I get you more coffee?" It's the part of a person that says, "Don't spank him; he was trying his best."

Now about the other Parent component, the Critical Parent. As I was growing up, I saw that the big people sometimes acted in a not-so-nurturing way. Since they knew what was right for everyone in the world, they noticed what people were doing wrong, and said so. This part of the Parent is the Critical Parent, or Punitive Parent.

The Critical Parent is authoritarian, worrisome, critical, vengeful, and prejudiced. "By golly, I know what you should be doing, and you aren't doing it. You're acting childish!" "Childish" is a Parent word: "I know what's 'mature,' and you're not it." Jesus never used the word "childish," but instead spoke of being childlike. Later I'll explore the difference. The Critical Parent is preoccupied with "shaping things up around here." "Sit up straight." "You look silly." "Don't talk with your mouth full—it's disgraceful!" (What's "disgraceful"? My hunch is that the parent's Child simply doesn't like it. I would prefer to tell my child that when he eats that way my stomach turns over and I want to throw up—and if he doesn't quit, I might well do that, all over the table. He'll get the point, and I will have told the truth.)

Some people spend a lot of their waking hours in their Parent ego state, particularly if their *role* requires it. Old-time preachers and priests and nuns were paid to nurture and criticize (always speaking from God's point of view, of course). Elementary-school teachers are expected to be pseudo-mothers. First sergeants are military mothers. "Stand up, sit down, shut up. You're not paid to think. Put on your winter blues. Quiet! I'll tell you when it's too hot to wear them."

You'll see a lot of Parents walking around once you start paying attention. I have a theory why there are so many. I think all adolescents experience a mild form of schizophrenia. They are busy trying on roles and choosing which pieces of themselves fit best. They're trying to resolve the mixed messages they've received at home and elsewhere. They're literally torn in two deciding what in the world they are going to be and do for the next sixty years. This shaky experience comes at a time when they need to feel some potency. The person who does not yet know how to be potent with all three of his ego states at once must choose among them, and because the Parent feels the most powerful, it's the one most frequently chosen.

Listen to a bunch of teen-agers. When they aren't happily letting their Kids out to play, they're total Parents—scolding, faultfinding, and busy with a heavy round of "Ain't it awful the way this school is run." I've seen scads of folk who are fourteen-going-on-ninety. And as they grow older, their choice of the Parent ego state as the "strongest" will become more confirmed.

People keep their Parent handy as a seemingly powerful protection for their Child. I say "seemingly" because the Parent rarely protects us. Yet at home or at a cocktail party, you'll observe Parents either at the ready or popping away.

Peter: "My tooth hurts."

Critical Father: "If you had brushed your teeth more often, it wouldn't hurt!"

How does dad know? He's an accountant, not a dentist.

There is another useful way to look at the Parent ego state. Our Parent tapes tell us not only how to parent other people but also how to parent ourselves. We call the Parent you send out to talk with the other folk your Active Parent. When you

nurture or criticize yourself, we refer to this as your Influencing Parent.

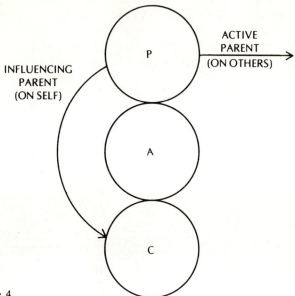

Figure 4

These two Parents can operate similarly or differently. For example, if you're late meeting me, my Active Parent might scold you and give you 500 reasons why you're a drag on the earth. If *I'm* late, however, my Influencing Parent may soothe and nurture me: "You couldn't help it, Artie. The traffic was bad. Anyway, you tried." Usually I see just the opposite happening. In most of my clients' heads the Parent excuses others while beating the daylights out of his own Child. I find it useful to note how the Parent operates in terms of self versus others.

Although Parent tapes are etched in acid on tungsten steel tapes by the time we are five or six, they do in fact change as we go through life. TA theory calls this Re-Parenting. Jacqui Schiff described the process in 1969 after using TA with schizophrenics—and curing them, although they had long been considered incurable. I recommend her book *All My Children* (see Bibliography).

The original tape is not erased, but is overpowered by the message of another and far more potent Parent. It happens this way: Your father always said that women were inferior. Later, a college dean whom you respect treats women as human beings, and four years of being around him re-etches your Parent tape. The new Parent-figure is so much more impressive on this subject than your father that it predominates.

Jesus had a powerful Active Parent. It was strong enough to overpower and replace the values and judgments stored in the Parent tapes of his disciples. Herein lies our hope for improving the quality of our tapes and subduing those that harm us instead of protecting us. It even suggests a reason for listening to powerful sermons. Unfortunately, really potent Active Parents are rare. One doesn't become potent by yelling louder and longer.

Our Parent tapes, then, represent a large complex of attitudes, values, judgments, opinions, and ways of acting and responding. The Parent ego state is an important, useful part of your makeup. But there's a hitch. To be useful, it must be checked against here-and-now reality. Unfortunately, when I'm in my Parent, I seldom think to check. "Why should I check when I'm already right?" Others can spot my Parent, but without a lot of practice I have trouble recognizing him. It takes practice and some help from outside. I suggest getting a Saint from your Private Church to perform this service for you until you get the hang of it—but only if he can do it without judging.

4
I Just Want the Facts, Ma'am

We have the Parent for storing our values and mustought-shoulds. We also have the capacity for collecting and processing facts. We don't always use this capacity, but it's there unless we've suffered brain damage or a birth defect. We call this part of our head—this ego state—the Adult. "Adult" doesn't mean the same thing as "mature." "Mature" is usually a Parent word: "I'll tell you what mature is. It's not laughing so loud. I know what mature is."

In our ego state symbol, the Adult breaks down like this:

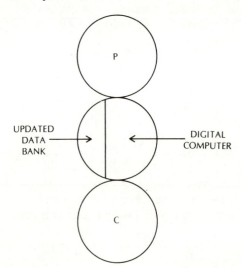

Figure 5

Eric Berne said that the Adult probably begins forming the moment the infant experiences a warm, moist, nurturing

breast in his mouth and realizes that food is coming. He has a
fact to process—nursing eliminates hunger pains. By the time
a child is five or six years old, he has a well-formed, func-
tioning Adult ego state. He won't be able to generalize or to
understand abstract things like "honor" or "love" for a few
more years, and his data bank isn't full—but he does have
one! (This might trigger some new thoughts and open some
new options for parents who are treating their children like
ding-a-lings.)

The Adult ego state is concerned only with facts; it doesn't
have opinions, feelings, value systems, or wants.* It just digs
data. Fact, fact, fact. *Click, click, click. Whirrrrrrr.* All day
long. "Three and three are six." "The sky is bluish-grayish-
yellowish-reddish." A good example of a "walking Adult
tape" is Mr. Spock, the guy with the pointy ears on television's
"Star Trek." He's always the unemotional dealer in data. You
spit in his face and he responds in a monotone, "Your spittle
is 98.763 degrees Fahrenheit and you appear to be displeased
with something I did."

The only "feeling" the Adult ever has is frustration. I
remember playing with one of those junior-grade computers.
It was fun to give it a problem it wasn't equipped to handle.
The thing would have a "nervous breakdown," whirring and
spitting and beating itself to death until I put it out o itst uugd
reeitiinini it t to o z eeerrrort.m... cCommmpptteeee g
guused.**

The Adult is similar to a digital computer in that it works in
linear fashion. Each successive fact is recorded and made to
fit (or not fit) with all the information already stored in the
Adult data bank. It receives its data from four sources.

*I disagree with the suggestion in Muriel James's and Dorothy Jongeward's *Born to
Win* that the Adult can imitate and/or incorporate a "new" Parent or Child. Many
people *get* in trouble by thinking that's what they're doing. I find it most helpful to
see the Adult as solely a fact-processor.

**The original copy read: "... I put it out of its misery by pulling the plug and reset-
ting it to zero. Computers get frustrated." As did this one! The publisher extends apol-
ogies for this gross but useful typo.

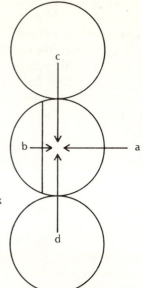

a. from the outside world
b. from its own updated data bank
c. from Parent tapes
d. from Child tapes

Figure 6

It is more accurate to say that the Adult *can* get information. Adult performance depends on how loudly the Adult tape is playing relative to the Parent and Child tapes. And how loudly each tape plays is influenced in turn by the importance that I assign it. Let's say I walk out on my front porch and see a tiger sitting under a tree one hundred yards away. My Child, understandably terrified of tigers, begins screaming "run, run, run" so loudly that my Adult can't "hear" the here-and-now information that the tiger is a long way off, is on a leash, has no teeth—is a stuffed tiger. My Child's fear has overwhelmed my Adult's logic, and my feet are doing their thing!

Mr. Jones, in a TA group for the first time, sits with his head bowed, wringing his hands. When I check with him, he explains he is terrified about being there. I ask him to look at all of the objects in the room. Then I ask him to take a long look at each person to spot anything that is "making him" terrified.

Typically he will find nothing. Usually, Mr. Jones's Parent or Child, or both, is having a fit inside him. For example, his parent is scaring him by saying, "Be careful! These people are sharp listeners and they will see right off what a dummy you are!" or "Don't admit you'd feel better if you knew more about them; if you do, they'll think you're pushy!" If these tapes play loudly enough, he will never collect the information he needs to solve his dilemma.

My invitation to look around gives Mr. Jones's Adult a chance to operate. Using his eyes to collect info gets him in touch with the *fact* that there's nothing in his here-and-now that's frightening, so he has to be frightening himself. This is a novel insight for many people. When they recognize they're doing it to themselves, they usually realize they can quit it if they want to. Many do. They usually pass it off with a comment like, "Having a chance to speak relieved the tension," but what really happened was they obtained useful information with their very own eyes, and their very own Adult processed it. Now they feel in control.

Learning to use our Adult—even when our Parent and our Child are screaming at each other—is vital. Only the Adult (computer) has the equipment to do four very important daily jobs: (1) estimate probabilities; (2) set priorities; (3) establish compromises when there is a conflict between choices; and (4) make the final decisions upon which we act.

Most of the time our Adult does this very well—we simply don't pay attention to how well we function. For example, you stand at a busy intersection. In a split second your Adult looks over the situation, counts the cars coming in all directions, notes which might turn, measures the distance to the opposite curb, gauges the speed of the cars, recalls how long it normally takes you to cross such a distance, and decides either to go or to wait. Now tell me you're a dingbat! If you think you are, you're working at it. The truth is that you use your Adult frequently—about many things.

My Parent can be changed only with difficulty ("I'm already updated, you pipsqueak!"), and my Child is current and impulsive ("I want it, and I want it right now"). My Adult, however, can be updated continuously. Example: My first day on the job, I look around and see a secretary. She's what grandma called "the wholesome type," which means she ain't gonna win a beauty contest. My computer goes *click* and records that I think the women in this office are homely. But a few minutes later a second lady walks by. Stunning! *"Click, click. Half* the women in this office are plain; *half* are beautiful." Each time new data are received, the percentages and categories change.

Some computer people have a word that I find useful in explaining why the Adult sometimes seems to malfunction. They call it GIGO ("Garbage In—Garbage Out"). My Adult-ego-state computer cannot create anything; it can only receive data, chew on them, reformulate them, and deal logically with them. Unless there's brain damage, everyone has an Adult and it's in good working order. Some Adults may work more quickly than others; some may have more facts stored; some may have been programed better by their families. But we all have one, and it's either being used or it isn't.

So when you do some thinking and the result is garbage, this doesn't mean that you have a sickly Adult. It means your Adult is getting bad information to work with. Several things could be happening. The Parent or the child, or both, could be feeding in hogwash that will never compute. Example: "I could be happy if my wife smiled more." That isn't a true statement; it's garbage coming from the Kid, who has decided to stay unhappy until she smiles on demand. Another: "When you let yourself enjoy life too much, something bad will happen." Parent trash! If either the Child or the Parent pollute the computer, bad decisions come out.

Another way to produce garbage is with "stimuli selec-tion." At any given moment you are bombarded by a jillion different stimuli to your eyes, ears, nose, fingers, skin, tongue. If you tried to pay attention to them all, you *would* go crazy. The same for trying to shut them all out. We need a balance. Early in life we learn to pick and choose the stimuli we're going to "listen" to. Have you ever driven down a street that you've traveled twice a day for years and suddenly spotted a "brand-new" twenty-year-old house? "Where did that come from?" It was there all the time, but you, for your own reasons, had not focused on it.

I suspect that the kinds and amounts of stimuli to which you give your attention depend on "permission." Some people enjoyed permission from their parental families to pay attention to useful things. Some have permission to pay attention to bad things only. Hypochondriacs can spot a pain in their innards two seconds before it hurts, yet choose to be totally unaware of a beautiful sunset. It depends on what we learn (or decide) to pay attention to. How we pay attention makes a difference in how we think. Therapy often takes place when a person is given permission (by others or himself) to pay attention to things or see them in a different way.

You have the capacity to set the volume of your ego states wherever you want, or switch them off. The control is in your head, and you already know how to operate it. Let me demonstrate: Your two-year-old is tugging at the draperies, so you move into your Parent and say sweetly, "Sammy, dear, be a good boy and don't do that to the nice draperies." Tug, tug, tug. You turn up the volume a notch. "Sammy, I said stop it." Tug, tug. "Samuel, stop it this instant!" (You know he hears you because you see your neighbor picking up her phone to call the police.) Now full volume, *"Samuel Constantine Fangschleister, one more tug and Mommy will break your arm!"* The pressure of the sound turns his muscles to jelly and he quits. You are delighted with the "effectiveness" of your screaming. Some folk are so pleased they decide to leave the volume up.

I have a theory that there is more than a volume control; there's also an automatic compensator in the output system of our sound amplifier. If we don't pay attention to what one of our ego states is saying at the moment, it *automatically* begins moving to a higher volume until we hear it and either respond or use our "manual override" to shut it back down. The sooner we pay attention with our Adult to what our Parent and Child are saying, the sooner we can take appropriate action.

So much for the machine in our heads. Let's move on to a more comprehensive look at the part of us that is the most fun, the most troublesome, and the most necessary—the Kid!

5

Of Such Is the Kingdom

In the Greek Orthodox Church they refer to the Patriarch as "first among equals." In TA theory the Child is equal to the other two ego states (in the healthy individual). In my way of thinking the Child is somehow "more equal" than the others, because the Child is where the real action is.

Like the Parent, the Child is an "archaic" ego state. And, like the Parent, it represents some 25,000 hours of input recorded during those first five or six years of your life. These Child tapes recorded what you experienced *inside,* whereas the Parent recorded things going on *outside.* You imprinted on your Child tapes how it felt to *be* a little no-necked monster in the land of the giants. You imprinted the decisions you made about who you were and how you would act.

The first nine months of your existence were pretty neat. Life was great in that indoor heated swimming pool. Food was pipelined to you, and you didn't have to swallow. There were a few bothersome jolts, but you got even with a few quick kicks of your own. On balance, it was a fine existence. Then came the earthquake. The bottom dropped out. The temperature fell. Some clown was clutching you. He may even have spanked you. Today you realize he was getting you to breathe, but at the time it was one helluva experience, and the experience (with all its shock) is stored somewhere in your Child tapes.

They gave you a pair of clean pants to wear, and you proceeded to dirty them. You couldn't feed yourself; you could only express rage when the food wasn't delivered quickly enough. When you tried to feed yourself you missed. The big folk communicated with each other, and they tried to talk with you. You tried to talk back, but the best you could do was to produce *"nooney, nonney, noney,"* which didn't even make sense to even you. There was a dark room without other people near. Later, uncles threw you into the sky to make you laugh, but you cried.

Looming even larger was your gut-level understanding that these big folk could get rid of you anytime they wanted just by stepping on your head! Or cutting off your milk. There are a lot of life-and-death feelings stored on your Child tapes.

A lot of good times are recorded there, too. People tickled your tummy and you giggled. (I'll bet you still giggle the same way unless your Parent has beaten the stuffin' out of your Kid.) There were warm breasts to nuzzle, tasty food to swig, and strong protective arms that said, "Everything will be OK." There was the good feeling of fingers spreading the baby oil and powder over your body, including the parts between your legs.

For the next five years or so you stored a lot of tapes in your Child ego state—tapes that said, "Here is what it is like for *me* to exist." And that same little five-year-old is still with you. Let's look at him more closely.

As Berne and his colleagues began studying the Child in their patients, they noticed a second Parent-Adult-Child model *within the Child,* three distinct facets to the Child ego state. In TA literature this Little Parent, Little Adult, and Little Child are labeled P_1, A_1, and C_1 (they are the originals) to differentiate them from the major ego states.* This system will interest you only if you have a "thing" about letters with little numbers after them or are going to research the field. We have some good names for the Three Kids!

Let's begin with the bottom circle in Figure 7, the Natural Child. (In early America "natural child" signified a child born illegitimately—which is appropriate here, for this is the part of you that "just happened.") The Natural Child may also be tagged the Free Child, the Happy Child, the OK Child, or the Fun-Lovin' Kid.

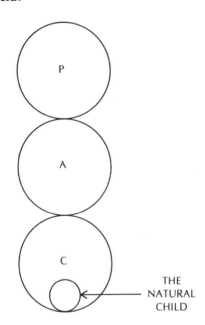

Figure 7

THE
NATURAL
CHILD

---

*I deliberately choose to blend the structural/developmental model (P_1, A_1, C_1) with the functional model (Adapted Child, Natural Child). While the structural/functional distinctions are important to developmental psychologists, theoreticians, and other scientists, I find they add to the layman's confusion. I choose to dwell on the great similarities I see between, say, A_1 and the Little Professor, etc.

This is the part of you that simply lives. He doesn't care what is good or bad; he simply knows what he likes and doesn't like. The Natural Child may like to cram lima beans up one nostril to see if they'll come out the other. It's the part of you that loves the taste of peanut butter (or broccoli, if you're that way). He likes to go into the bathroom, lock the door, put water in the tub, climb in, lie down, and make his tummy go up and down because he loves the way the water runs over his belly button.

A Natural Child loves to:
- Smell flowers
- Walk through mud puddles with his shoes on so that he can feel the warm squish-squish
- Fondle his "thing" and other people's
- Make noise for the sheer joy of hearing the sound
- Lie in the grass and look up at the fluffy clouds and spot horsies (unless you're like the kid in "Peanuts" who, instead of horsies, sees "The Battle of Balaclava")

These are my examples. Your Kid has her own list.

The Natural Child isn't all fun and joy, however. Since this is the part of you that feels and experiences life around you, he necessarily pays attention to things he doesn't like, too. My Natural Child doesn't like big, scary noises, or being left alone for too long a time, or broccoli (even with cheese), or getting hit in the stomach. These things disturb me, not because they're "wrong" but because I simply don't like them, even if my Parent says I should.

Since the Natural Child is the origin of most of your genuine feelings, he's a very important part of you. If you're ever going to enjoy anything in this life, your Child ego state will have the experience. Your Parent gets a modicum*of "enjoyment" out of nurturing other people or criticizing them; it gets a smidgin of satisfaction out of being obeyed and a bit out of remembering. Your Adult "enjoys" clicking out the data and fitting the pieces together. But neither has the Child's capacity for ecstasy. For example, can you picture two computers making

* small amount

love to each other? Can you picture two Critical Parents having sex? ("Don't enjoy it so much; it isn't ladylike.") The Natural Child is our primary receiver of joy. "Unless you become as Little Children," you won't even *understand* that there *is* a Kingdom of Heaven, let alone *find* it.

The second part of the Child ego state is equally important to making it in this world. Rather than use the academic-sounding term "Adult in the Child," I prefer to call it the "Little Professor."*

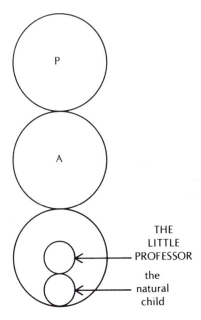

Figure 8

THE
LITTLE
PROFESSOR

the
natural
child

When you were birthed you had no Adult to think for you, yet you needed to figure things out. God (or Nature, if you're still insisting that *we're* all there is) gave your Child a

*I sometimes use the term "Smart-assed Kid" with people who enjoy all kinds of words, the point being that we have a highly creative talent that won't let society's disapproval destroy a good idea. Parents seldom like "smart asses."

miniature computer to serve until the big one came on back order. This computer is not a linear computer that works by adding facts together; it's more like an analogue computer, programed to pick out a particular grouping of data (an "image" or a "gestalt") from a whole mess of information. This computer looks for, and signals the presence or absence of, a particular conglomeration.

This capacity is sometimes referred to as "intuition," but I don't think that really captures its scope. We're talking about a very clever little boy or girl who can have instant "hunches" about data. For instance, have you ever, on the edge of your vision, glimpsed a person flashing by and known immediately which it was, male or female? Or who it was? If someone had asked you how you knew, you'd have been forced to say, "I don't know how I know, I just know." The logical process for dealing with fact-fact-fact data had not yet reached your Adult. Or, you enter a room full of strangers and instantly know which people will be friends and which you'll likely have trouble with? Your Little Professor is working all the time. He can spot the tiniest hints of body language. He looks for all the little clues that will give him insight into how he can make it in this World of Giants.

Because the Child tends to deal in life-or-death categories, the Little Professor works quickly. He knows instantly when something has gone wrong. He senses that things just aren't "right." He's not always accurate, but lots of times he's told he's wrong when he's absolutely right.

Scene: A youngster walks into his home. Dad is in the bathroom with the door closed; mom is peeling potatoes. His Little Professor *knows* something is wrong. They've had one of their Big Fights. "What's wrong, Mom?" he asks. "Nothing," she screams. "Go away!" After many of these scenes a person may decide to quit using his Little Professor—he's been told that the Little Professor makes mistakes when, in fact, he's right 85 percent of the time, which is a lot.

The Little Professor's forte is speed. When he *is* right, he delivers the message a long time before the Adult has enough facts to make a judgment. Let me show you how quickly he works. A client in one of my groups was having difficulty seeing a point I wanted him to understand. So I drew the three circles on the board (if only I had a dollar for every circle I've drawn) and wrote, using "earthy" language, what I felt each of his three ego states was saying. When I got to the Kid, I had written only part of the sentence when the client started to chuckle. His Little Professor had sped ahead, gotten the point, and thought it hilarious. But because this man had trouble letting his Child get a word in edgewise, he immediately squelched his laughter and went into his Adult. By the time I had finished writing, he was leaning forward and squinting, very serious about the whole thing. "I can't read your writing," he complained.

Much that we call hypocrisy is, in my mind, not hypocrisy at all, but a major disagreement between at least two of the ego states. In the example above, the man was *not* being two-faced. His Adult really *couldn't* read most of my handwriting, just snatches of it. But his Kid had been able to read enough to get the whole picture. Hypocrisy occurs when one ego state *lies,* which doesn't happen a lot. Usually it's my Parent and my Child who disagree. For example, my Parent thinks people are better off going to church. They *should* go! My Kid frequently gets little out of church services and likes to skip the whole thing. If you heard my Parent speak and then saw my Kid at the beach, you could call this "hypocrisy," but TA would say my Child had scored a victory against my Parent, right or wrong.

Your Little Professor knows *without thinking* exactly what to say to make your spouse climb the wall—or into your arms. He knows when you've been talking too much. Mrs. Brown came into our group and, as usual, began boring everyone to death. As we were getting in touch with how bored we really were, she glanced around and said, "I know I'm boring you, but . . ." And she continued to blab. But her Kid knew!

Your Little Professor is the source of your creativity and imagination. Little kids are creative, imaginative people, and so are you. The trouble is that most of us have shipped our Little Professor off to Siberia (along with the Natural Child) because others have convinced us it's "bad news." Without these two Child states we go through life complaining we're "dummies," and think we aren't creative or inventive like everyone else.

To its loss, society doesn't value the Little Professor, and yet it was a Little Professor who got us going to the moon. "Wouldn't it be sumpin," the scientist mused, "if we could tie a guy onto the end of a firecracker and boom him allll the wayyyy to the moon!" Then, after his Kid had thunk up this totally unreasonable idea (which would never have occurred to a computer), the scientist let his Adult figure out how to do it. Every scientific adventure begins with a wide-eyed little boy or girl wondering what would happen *if*—

As with other parts of your personality, your Little Professor can work against you. He is used by the Child to figure out *sneaky* ways of making it in the family. Thus the Little Professor is the inventor of all our "Games" and the one who can set you up for a Game in any situation you find yourself. A "Game" works like this: Someone says, "We'd like for you to go to the beach with us." Before any other part of you can respond, your Little Professor has found a way to turn this friendly act of inclusion into a Game of "Why Do People Always Leave Me Out?" Your Child pouts, "No! No one ever asks me where I want to go. I'll go to the movies—alone." Pout, pout. Your Little Professor is really good at helping you feel bad, if that's what you want.

Another important function of your Child is having fantasies and hunches. Sadly, Parent ego states and society in general disapprove of fantasies because they aren't "productive" or "real." The heck they aren't! When I'm working with someone, I let my Little Professor play with any idea he may have. He's wrong some of the time, but I have an Adult that can check his ideas and eliminate the mistakes. But most of the time my Little Professor comes up with some really unusual and accurate answers long before my Adult has begun to operate.

Out of these fantasies come hunches. Again, my hunches can be wrong, but far more often they're on target. Frequently, as I listen to someone relating a problem, I imagine how a kid would feel about that. Then I fantasize a situation that would make a child feel that way. For example, while discussing his guilt feelings over "controlling" his teen-agers, Mr. Fangschleister reports working all weekend on papers out of his attache case. My Little Prof immediately has a fantasy of a kid whose parents make him cut the grass while all the other kids are going swimming. He's hot, lonesome, and feeling put-upon. His allowance won't be increased a penny for all his extra work. He'll never ever get to live that day over. When I tell Mr. F. my fantasy, he immediately responds, "That's exactly how I felt!" He now has a good idea why he was so crabby with his offspring: It was that paperwork.

I can't praise this little guy enough. He is indestructible. Even when you've locked him up in the basement, he has already discovered an emergency exit through the coal chute and is out helping you figure out how to cope. But your disowning him makes his work harder. He had to do all this without your "knowledge" (without having been considered by your Adult), so he engages in guerrilla warfare to achieve his goal.

The third part of the Child, the Parent in the Child, originally served to protect you. This part of your Child said in effect, "I'll do anything I have to do, no matter how crazy it is, in order to make it around here! And I'll listen to the other Kids for instructions."

In TA circles this part of the Child is called the "Adapted Child," because it's the piece of us that thinks he has to adapt to everything.

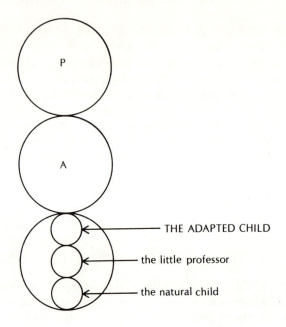

THE ADAPTED CHILD

the little professor

the natural child

Figure 9

The term "Adapted Child" is OK for learned journals, but I prefer "Crazy Kid." It captures this part of me better. This is the part of me that insists on doing stuff that is just plain crazy. I use "crazy" here to mean something that has no connection to the reality around it—like putting on three fur coats when the temperature is 110.

I'd like to talk about "crazy" for a tad. Since we've gotten more "sophisticated" as a society, we have stopped using this word except as a Parental put-down. Our Adult used terms like "mentally ill," which I think is a change for the worse. "Mentally ill" implies defective machinery and irrevocable doom. True, some "mental illnesses" are undoubtedly caused by faulty genes, adverse chemical changes in the brain, and such, but the implication that it's our head that's sick provides a terrific cop-out for the person with the problem and imposes a terrific handicap on the person treating him. If a professional has proclaimed me "mentally ill," I can play a heavy game of "If It Weren't for You (You Nasty Bug in My Head That Makes Me Act the Way I Do)." I can keep on doing crazy stuff. Even the doctor will agree I'm pitiful.

I remember that a decade or so ago people bragged about how neurotic they were. Boy, was "neurotic," a magical word! If I am a certified "neurotic," I can get away with darned near anything. "Don't ask me to do that; I'm a very nervous person." What we're really talking about, I think, is a piece of us that is *willing* to do crazy things if he *needs* to (or thinks he needs to).

The Crazy Kid/Adapted Child *feels* like something beyond our control. He is very much under our control, doing things that *he* has "learned" will help him survive. He follows a "script" and not the here-and-now. So the Crazy Kid does things out of the blue that are totally inappropriate to the situation. He gets us into trouble at the drop of a hat. He pours sugar in gas tanks, punches extra holes in IBM cards, and generally makes our lives miserable. Not knowing that this part of us is at work, we tend to assume that there really is a Wicked Witch of the West, and it's all her fault. "It certainly wasn't *my* idea to get sick just before the examination. I love school! It's just that *I always* get sick before a test."

Some examples of "crazy." You old-timers will remember how it was twenty years ago when we had to go to church in August and there wasn't any air conditioning. It was hot! (Sermons on hell really came through.) The only air stirring came from those cardboard fans graciously given the church by the deacon, who laid people away for a living. There we sat, dressed to the "nines." Women in their slips—and girdles—and long hose—and—and—and then a hat on top. They covered themselves with powder as a final hope for stanching the mighty flow of sweat. The men wore vests. In summer! And a coat to make sure they'd be too hot. They half-strangled themselves with a tie. (I can get some jollies any time I want by picturing the archaeologists of the next era trying to deal with our compulsion to wear ties. "Let's see. They hung this piece of cloth around their necks and then—[shocked]—then they did *what*?")

It was insane! Crazy! But we did it because our Crazy Kid said, "That's what a guy has to do around here to make it." Our Parent supports such decisions by providing a philosophical and religious rationale: "We dress up to show our respect for the Lord."

Or, how many of you have endured a meeting while your bladder expanded and expanded. As the meeting goes on and on, your bladder starts to feel like a basketball, but you remain seated because you don't want to interrupt the group. "People might be irritated." Worse, "They'll know where I'm going, and I don't want them to know I have to do it too." So you sit and rely on religion, which is what mom told you to do in times of trial: "Please, dear God, make him end his speech before I explode and drown everybody." We don't explode, so we keep on doing this waiting to the detriment of our plumbing. If you leave, you aren't likely to miss anything; besides, you ought to take care of yourself, but your Crazy Kid sits there and suffers because he'll do anything he's supposed to do. Being crazy has gotten him this far.

I remember a training group at Anita Plummer's house.* She's the TA guru who taught most of us in Houston how to apply TA theory to therapy. Just as she began talking, Person A in the circle spotted a TA journal she wanted to examine. Her Adapted Child was well trained in not bothering people, so she whispered to Person B, "Get that journal with the red cover for me, will you?" Person B turned to Person C and passed on the message. Each person waited for an appropriate time to whisper. After a while every Little Professor had picked up the commotion. Anita stopped her dialogue and used this as an illustration of the Crazy Kid. It would have

---

*Anita Plummer, M.S.W., is a Teaching Member in ITAA and my own TA mentor. She's a fantastically creative therapist. "Guru," by the way, is *my* fun-word, and not a proper designation.

been less disruptive to have said, "Hey, excuse me, but before you begin would someone pass me that magazine?" A ten-second interruption instead of a two-minute one.

The Crazy Kid is untouched by reality. He simply doesn't listen much to outside stimuli. Remember Mr. Jones, the one I asked to look around at the group to see what was terrifying him? His Crazy Kid was in charge; he hadn't bothered to check the facts because he already knew what he was supposed to do. Father always said, "Strange groups are scary."

Untouched by reality, yet needing to respond to something, the Crazy Kid listens to Parent tapes instead of the here-and-now. He's aided by one other "source" of information: injunctions. During your first five years you heard a lot from those around you. "Cross your legs." "Close your mouth when you chew gum." "Don't pull the cat's tail." All of this was dutifully stored in your Parent ego state, or, if a fact ("The stove is hot"), in your Adult. You heard all these admonitions; still, your Child wanted to know the straight skinny.

Let me use military life as an analogy. When a unit goes to a new base, the commander or his representatives (all of them Parents) give the newcomers a long list of the rules and regulations. Then, after the "lecture," the serviceman goes out to get the "real poop." He heads for the Airman's Club, where the other Kids are gathered. "Hey! How long can you stretch a pass around here before they get bothered? How tough is the Old Man, really? What are the chances for . . . ?" Now he's getting the information that *matters*. From the other Kids.

In your first home you were like the new soldier. What did the other Kids have to say? You looked at mom's Child and dad's Child and asked, "Hey, you guys, I've heard your proclamations, but what do you *really* want me to do?" And they told you. We tend to forget that although we're acting very "adult and grown-up" (as when we're trying to impress our offspring), our Child ego state is playing all around us. Everyone can see the Child but us. "I am *not* angry! I am just yelling because you are so %#&$ obstinate!" You listened to your parents' Kids!

Here's how it works. Dad really loves little Janie. He wants her to amount to something. "Use your head, honey; it will be important to you in later life." Parent to Parent. He has said it a thousand times. Janie notices, however, that every time she does use her head and gets it right, the edges of dad's mouth turn down in the slightest hint of a pout. His Child is disappointed. "How can I be the daddy if she does it for herself?" Dad doesn't stay in the Child long, even though that's where his feelings are. He quickly slips back into his Adult or Parent and praises her to high heaven. But meanwhile she noticed the glimmer from his Kid, and her own Crazy Kid comes up with a crazy translation: "It really makes dad happy when I don't think. What dad is *really* saying to me is, 'Don't think, Janie.' " She fears dad will go away if she doesn't act dumb and please him.

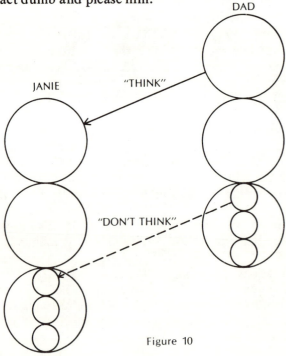

Figure 10

Forty-five years later Janie is still faithfully following the "injunction" (that's what we call these secret messages between the Kids of our parents and us). What does she do with his Parent-to-Parent message "Think"? She has a couple of choices. She can scold herself for not thinking and look forward to a day when she finally gets it right, or she can spend eighteen hours a day covered with sweat trying to give birth to a thought without producing one. In either case she is obeying the message from the other Kids, who told her how to get along in that family.

Injunctions come in many forms, depending on how the Crazy Kid heard them: Don't exist, don't enjoy life, don't be yourself, don't show your emotions, don't be happy, don't be successful, don't be attractive, don't surpass me—and so on.* When the Crazy Kid decides he has heard the message right, he makes decisions about how he will carry out the "orders."

One gal in our group was really gorgeous. Also bright, witty, and charming. But also nine kinds of "hung-up." She absolutely wouldn't admit that she was good-looking or talented. As time passed, we learned why: Her mother's Child had indicated that the daughter was never to surpass the mother. Since her mother was only "average," the daughter felt she had to go through life with her brakes on. The slightest gut feeling that she was showing up her mother (or anyone else) caused fantastic problems inside her.

I'm sure her mother never wanted her daughter to be a nobody. Mom's Child, however, looked at this beautiful baby

---

*Bob and Mary Goulding (M.D. and M.S.W., respectively, and both Teaching Members in ITAA), TA pioneers and founders and directors of the Western Institute for Group and Family Therapy, say there are ten basic injunctions:

Don't!	Don't be important.
Don't be!	Don't be well/sane.
Don't be close.	Don't belong
Don't be you.	Don't make it.
Don't grow up.	Don't be important.

All other injunctions can be fitted into these ten.

girl and said, "Oh, when everyone sees how pretty Janie is they won't pay attention to me!" Janie could tell that her mom's Kid wasn't pleased when Janie really looked good, and she gave in to the survival demand. Now, years later, she is dutifully (and very crazily) reporting, "I am *not* pretty. Sometimes when I look into a mirror I can't believe how ugly I am."

It might help to know that there are three forms of the Crazy Kid. Which you have chosen for your own depends on the messages you got from your family and how you learned "to make it" in that group. Eric Berne originally termed these varieties the "Prick," the "Jerk," and the "Sulk."

The Prick (or "Socker," as Solon Samuels calls him) is given to understand he will make it at home if he is helpful. He is expected to be a winner, but the definition of "winning" comes from the family. By the time he is three years old, he is being asked to make decisions: "Should we go to New York or San Francisco this summer, Little Prick?" He replies, "We go to New York!" thinking anything "new" is better than "sand." "Should we," asks mom, "have veal scallopini or beef stroganoff?" The Kid speaks neither Italian nor Russian, but he's supposed to make a decision (the right decision), and so he votes for the scallopini, whatever that is!

Years later the Little ******* is still "running things." He operates from the "I'm OK, you're Not OK" position. He makes decisions and gets things done. "If I don't do it, it won't be done."

Of the three forms of adaptation that Crazy Kids undertake, this probably is the most useful to society. Then why am I "scolding" it? This individual is a "winner" because he *has* to be. He's acting the way he is supposed to act to "keep from destroying himself." He has no permission to reply, "Frankly, mom, I don't care what we eat." He must be a Decider, a Doer. Years later he winds up the president of a PTA that he says he can't stand, the treasurer of a company he says is wearing him out, and the head deacon in a church that preaches things he doesn't believe in. Friends and relatives say about him, "Sure, he's a ***, but we couldn't do without him." He believes that if he fails to produce, he will be "worthless." He usually dies at an early age.*

When the Little Prick is impressing people, he feels good. He's "on top of things." If, on the other hand, he is not impressing everyone, he gets depressed. "I've got to please *everyone* (to please Mom)!" Two things keep him at least a little depressed: (1) Obviously he can't impress everyone he meets; and (2) in many cases he doesn't have permission to ask people what they expect; he has to show off "blindly."

The Jerk (or "Sobber") resembles the Prick in his emphasis on winning, except the Jerk usually fails. He operates from the "I'm Not OK, you're OK" position. He thinks his parents will love him more if he *tries* very, very hard, and *fails*. "Carry the plates to the table, Little Jerk, *and don't drop them!*" No instruction is ever given him without a caution. When the Jerk hears this enough times, he gets the picture. "If I wasn't supposed to drop the plates, she wouldn't keep telling me not to." He drops them. He overhears the parents telling their cocktail guests, "Yes, our Johnny tries so hard, but he never makes it." He must be getting it right! Otherwise they wouldn't be "bragging" about him.

Years later the Jerk is working sixteen hours a day but is passed over for promotions. He makes just enough mistakes to insure his failing, but is seldom fired. How can you fire someone who is constantly covered with sweat from trying?

The Jerk spends a lot of time sobbing. "Why does it always work out wrong for me? I'll never get it right (promise, promise!)" He decides to seek help, then carefully chooses an impotent therapist who won't cure him. His favorite phrase is "I'm really trying hard."

The third way to adapt (and the third version of the Crazy Kid) is to sulk. In some families children get the idea they're

---

*See Amy Harris' beautiful exploration of this in her article, "Good Guys and Sweethearts," *Transactional Analysis Journal*, II, no. 1 (January 1972), 13-18.

supposed to handle problems by pouting. "Don't you dare go to your room and pout (like you always do)." So Sulk goes into his room and pouts. It's expected of him. Dad comes and beats on the door. "Come out of that room this instant." The Sulk knows dad doesn't really want him out of the room—dad's 36 years old and weighs 193 pounds, and if he wanted him out, he would *get* him out. A smashed door panel would be a small price to pay. Dad screams for a while, then leaves, defeated. Sulk's behavior is confirmed.

Years later Sulk is still going to his room and sulking—even if it has to be a room in the back of his head. One TA trainer says the model of the Sulk is a person standing on a busy street corner in a suit of armor with the visor pulled down. Once every two weeks he opens the visor wide enough and long enough to shout, "Go to hell," and then snaps it back shut.

So there you have it. The Child in all his glory. He's many-faceted. He's unique. He's enjoyable and fun—and the seat of our internal problems. In most of us the Child has been bent and twisted to conform to "society" (Parents); he has been ignored and ill-used, locked up in the basement. Many grown-ups refuse to admit there's a piece of them that is, in fact, only five years old. Those who refuse are never in touch with what I maintain to be the most important part of their personality. When they're in trouble, they can't deal with the problem because they wouldn't talk to a "Kid" even if he did exist in them. Problem or no problem, they can't be in touch with the joy, the imagination, the creativity, or the here-and-now "wisdom" of their Child ego state. It's a pity!

6
What Do You Do with an Ego State?

Now that you know about ego states, what can you do with them? For starters, you can become proficient at "spotting" an ego state.* It takes time and practice, as does learning to ride a bike. There's a risk that just as you start getting good at it, you'll become sick of it all, as with high-school French. The secret of success is hanging in there until you are past the "I'm sick of it" stage.

Once you master this new skill, you can be selective about when you use it. For the most part, I only look for ego states when there's something troublesome going on, or when I'm working. Unless you're getting practice, I don't think it's either profitable or fun to watch for ego states at a bridge game, when you could be enjoying yourself. Too much explaining can destroy life's poetry. (I'll never forgive whoever it was who taught me the scientific explanation of a rainbow.) If, however, a fight were to break out among the players and spoil your enjoyment, ego-state spotting could be a useful tool.

You will find "laboratory" material everywhere, whether you're with someone or alone. Use your Adult fact finder to spot ego states. As you progressively increase the amount of time you spend in your Adult each day, you'll become more proficient at summoning it whenever you want it to work. That's a good feeling all by itself!

---

*I've left out "how to spot an ego state." Most other books describe this well, e.g., *Born to Win*, by James and Jongeward, and *I'm OK—You're OK* by Harris.

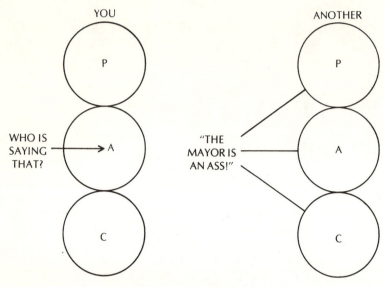

Figure 11

OK. You're getting adept at spotting ego states, especially in yourself. Now there's a fun thing you can do, if you want, with your very own ego states. You can begin using all six pieces of yourself. (If you don't recall what the six are, refer to Figure 12.)

This is important. Most folk have been brainwashed into thinking they are clods who don't have much on the ball. When a person becomes aware he has at *least* six "answers" for any given problem, he tends to feel better about himself right away! Remember, anxiety goes down as options increase.

Let's say your wife always squeezes the toothpaste tube in the middle. This either irritates your Parent (who knows the "right" way to squeeze tubes) or your Kid (because your Parent forces you to resqueeze the tube before you can brush your own teeth). You want to take some effective action. Let me illustrate what the six-pack approach might do about that.

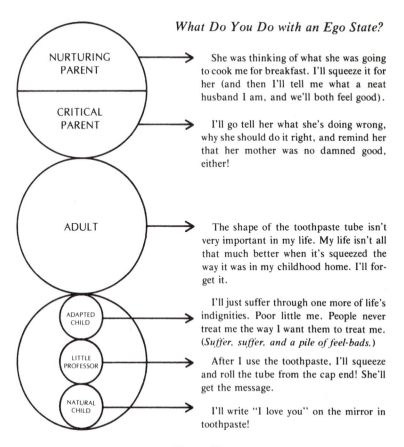

She was thinking of what she was going to cook me for breakfast. I'll squeeze it for her (and then I'll tell me what a neat husband I am, and we'll both feel good).

I'll go tell her what she's doing wrong, why she should do it right, and remind her that her mother was no damned good, either!

The shape of the toothpaste tube isn't very important in my life. My life isn't all that much better when it's squeezed the way it was in my childhood home. I'll forget it.

I'll just suffer through one more of life's indignities. Poor little me. People never treat me the way I want them to treat me. (*Suffer, suffer, and a pile of feel-bads.*)

After I use the toothpaste, I'll squeeze and roll the tube from the cap end! She'll get the message.

I'll write "I love you" on the mirror in toothpaste!

Figure 12

So! Six "answers" to my "problem" already. Toothpaste tubes usually aren't a big problem, but if they were for me and I didn't like any of the answers above, I could go back around for six more options and then choose the one that is most effective and most pleasing.

The Critical Parent and the Adapted Child usually come up with the least helpful, least useful ideas. Critical Parents bitch, nag, push, and shove. Adapted Children "try to get it right," and end up sulking, pouting, or "trying to" again, only harder. Neither spends any time in the here-and-now.

Both consistently follow worn-out and unproductive patterns. Yet most folk tend to rely on the one or the other to "solve" *all* their problems. Unfortunately, the more time we spend in these unuseful ego states, the less time we have to use and enjoy our other four ego states.

For practice, I'm going to do this one more time with another problem: sons and daughters who litter the living room with shoes, books, horns, pencils, makeup, empty coke bottles, chewing-gum wrappers, chewing gum!

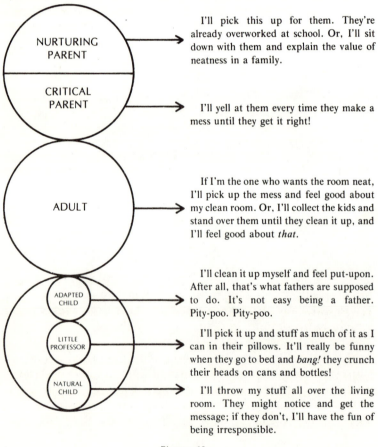

NURTURING PARENT → I'll pick this up for them. They're already overworked at school. Or, I'll sit down with them and explain the value of neatness in a family.

CRITICAL PARENT → I'll yell at them every time they make a mess until they get it right!

ADULT → If I'm the one who wants the room neat, I'll pick up the mess and feel good about my clean room. Or, I'll collect the kids and stand over them until they clean it up, and I'll feel good about *that*.

ADAPTED CHILD → I'll clean it up myself and feel put-upon. After all, that's what fathers are supposed to do. It's not easy being a father. Pity-poo. Pity-poo.

LITTLE PROFESSOR → I'll pick it up and stuff as much of it as I can in their pillows. It'll really be funny when they go to bed and *bang!* they crunch their heads on cans and bottles!

NATURAL CHILD → I'll throw my stuff all over the living room. They might notice and get the message; if they don't, I'll have the fun of being irresponsible.

Figure 13

You may have some difficulty distinguishing between the Critical Parent and the Adapted Child. The difference is, the Parent *gives* the orders; the Adapted Child either obeys them or rebels against them.

At puberty many compliant children decide to become "independent." Mothers and fathers report, "We can't do a thing with him! He always does the opposite of what we tell him." Sure! The Adapted Child always operates in terms of "instructions from a Parent." Once he understands the "orders," he has two alternatives. He can adapt by complying or he can adapt by rebelling. In either case he is still chained to the order; he makes his decisions only *after* someone tells him what he is "supposed to do." When father's Critical Parent yells, "You still haven't cut the grass. Hop to it!" Sammy's Rebellious Child responds, "I will—sometime," and heads for the nearest pinball machine. (He had been looking for something to do, but now that dad wants him to cut the grass, he "has to refuse" if he is to show his independence. Some "independence"!)

Usually the Critical Parent and the Adapted Child go hand in hand. The Adapted Child says, "I'm supposed to stand up straight," and either does or doesn't, depending on whether he's into compliance or rebellion. He always acts in response to the Critical Parent in his head, who yells, "Stand up straight, you dummy! Want people to *know* what an ass you are?" (The Adapted Kid *feels* like an ass; the Critical Parent keeps reminding him he *is* one!)

The Adapted Child's tendency to *act like* a Parent sometimes causes a spotter to confuse the two. You've seen a four-year-old wearing a long dress and mommy's high heels. The Adapted Child often acts the same way, even in forty-year-old folk. What is missing is the *potency* of the Parent. When the Parent ego state issues a command, the Child usually hops to, but Adapted Children can only "try" to be potent by *acting like* a daddy. We call this "playing Parent."

Picture this: Dad, in a slight whine, is talking to the youngsters. "You know how hard Daddy tries to do the right thing. You really should be more polite and considerate. After all, blah, blah, blah." His progeny stand there and nod because he's bigger than they are, but nobody is taking him seriously. His Adapted Child is "playing Parent" again. They can see how he's rocking up on his heels to borrow height. When his real Parent begins to shout, they listen carefully.

As dad talks, you can hear the Parent in his head shouting out the commands: "Tell them how hard you try.... Now tell them they should be considerate.... Now tell them ..." His Adapted Child (who wants to be a good daddy if only he can) puts on his father's vest, complete with watch, chain, and fob, and acts out the role. The last stage of his performance is to wonder why it never works.

Ego states are not always as easily spotted as I've implied. Sometimes the waters are muddy. In some folk you can't *find* all three ego states. There's a reason.

In TA diagraming the "healthy" or "normal" person looks like this:

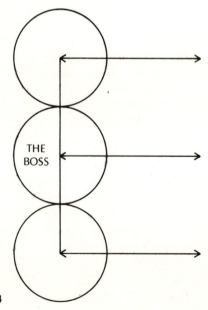

Figure 14

The fully functional person will have three distinct and operational ego states and be able to move from one to another at will. Most important, the Adult will retain "executive control," meaning he will call the shots, will make the decisions, and will tell the Parent and Child when they get to perform. The healthy person uses his Adult to keep him in touch with the constantly changing here-and-now situation so he (the Adult) can send out the appropriate ego state to deal with it.

Most of us seldom have all three "distinct and operational ego states." Eric Berne noted two pathological conditions, which he called "contamination" and "exclusion."

When two ego states overlap, contamination occurs. For example, either the Parent or Child, or both, can invade the Adult computer and contaminate the computations. Contamination occurs when either the Parent's value system and opinions or the Child's feelings and decisions are taken to be factual.

The Parent says, "I believe women are less intelligent than men." This is a value judgment based on bad information, and it demonstrates that the Parent is contaminating the Adult. Contamination may lead to this picture:

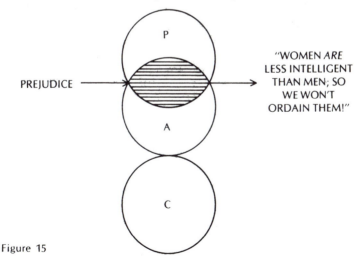

PREJUDICE

"WOMEN *ARE* LESS INTELLIGENT THAN MEN; SO WE WON'T ORDAIN THEM!"

Figure 15

Another example of contamination: The Child says, "I'm scared of all these people! What if they won't like me?" The Child is contaminating the Adult. It looks like this:

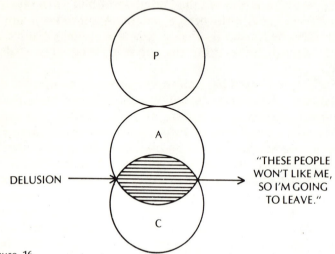

Figure 16

As the drawings show, Parent contamination produces prejudice, while Child contamination produces delusions. Both produce the "crazies," which can lead us to trouble. In sorting out the pieces of our lives, it's important for us to identify the "crazies" that we have in our head. We should at least *know* that what we're hearing are Parent or Child tapes, not data that the Adult can compute.

Until we've named our particular "crazies," there is no way to get rid of them. A young woman was having problems communicating with her husband, and no wonder! She had some crazies. She reported from her Parent-contaminated Adult "My folks were such great people that all my Parent tapes are good!" A double whammy! She had used her Parent to evaluate her Parent tapes. Tilt!

Only the computer-like Adult can check out Parent tapes against here-and-now realities and be accurate about it. Yet a common way to get into, and stay in, trouble is to measure the validity of our Parent tapes with our own Parent! Especially in the church. Example: We have perpetuated the myth that it is wrong to avoid suffering and right to avoid money. If this is questioned, we *prove* our stand by pointing out that "God wants us to suffer, because, like fine gold, the heat eliminates impurities—and the love of money is the root of all evil." We even quote the passages (without understanding that it is a Parent tape that has given worth to Scripture). I know that sometimes suffering can be used to learn; but I'm also aware that in many cases suffering *destroys* more than it creates. I know that for some people too much money is the root of trouble, but that for over half the world it is not the love of money but the *lack* of it that leads to evil.

Let me cite another type of Parent-contamination that has been reinforced by the church. St. Paul said to the Romans, "Do not be conceited or think too highly of yourself; but think your way to a sober estimate." The caution against self-adulation can be defended as an Adult-to-Adult statement. When I overestimate my abilities I can drown in the misery that follows. If you doubt this, watch what happens when a drunk overestimates his ability to fly and steps off the thirtieth floor. But Paul's statement has been read by later Christians as a Parental command, "Don't think you're too hot, and *I'll* tell you what too much is!" Contamination of the Adult by the Parent. Many Christians are ready to declare that *any* self-regard is too much. They spend their time poor-mouthing themselves. Underestimating your abilities is neither modesty nor Christian humility. It's crazy! It's crazy because it is "not reality."

As we will see later, this contaminated "fact" of my worthlessness and inability to control my life or thoughts condemns me to feel unloved forever.

Down through the centuries contamination has served the church poorly. One sort of contamination tends to cycle:

CHURCH'S PARENT: If you're not careful of God's power, you're going to lose it, dummy!

CHURCH'S CHILD: Oh, I don't want to lose it! I know what I'll do. I'll put it in a Mason jar like I did a butterfly one time. There! Now I'll store it in a nice safe where I keep my rituals and laws and doctrines and holy papers. Now I won't lose it.

(*Years later*)

WORLD'S ADULT: I don't see any life in your butterfly. It looks dead to me.

CHURCH'S CHILD: It is not dead. I know it's alive, because it was alive when I put it in there! So there!

CHURCH'S PARENT: The Kid's right. He did it just the way I told him to, and it's the only right way!

The Parent's opinion that locking *anything* up keeps it safe is taken as fact. The Child's belief in the "magic" of his jar agrees with the Parent's opinion. Between them they resist the information that their butterfly isn't moving anymore.

Two words suggestive of contamination by the Child are "can't" and "have to." I hear them a lot. Most of the "can'ts" are really "won'ts." Mrs. Smith says, "I can't tell my husband that he's getting fatter than a pig!" Wrong-o! The fact is that she *won't* tell him. She has *decided* not to tell him because he will hit her in the mouth, and chewing with welded dentures is tough. She likes to *think* she is incapable, and the result of this crazy contamination is feeling helpless. Instead of feeling helpless, she could pat herself on the back for knowing how to stay out of trouble. She could buy a big mirror and put it opposite the spot where he undresses at night. Instead, she complains of her "helplessness."

The term "have to" is also contaminated and is equally destructive. There are very few "have-to's" in all of life, death being the only one I can think of at the moment. A kid told me the other day he "had to" go to school. He was feeling bad about how put-upon he was. Actually he had made a decision to go to school. His allowance was contingent upon his school attendance, and he had looked over the options and *decided* that going to school was the best deal. He had overlooked yet another option—going to school *and* finding a way to enjoy himself. He had decided on feeling put-upon.

I have a theory about how contamination begins. Mom tells Sally Sue, aged four, to get dressed for the party. Sally Sue has a developing Adult ego state, and she uses it to plan her wardrobe. She figures she needs something to cover her bottom, so she puts on the ruffled panties of her swimsuit. "Now," she says determinedly, "I need to cover my top." She pulls on her prettiest pajama top. She knows mom likes her to wear shoes to parties, so she puts on her tap-dancing slippers. But when she displays herself to mommy, who has been fantasizing swirls of loveliness, *bang!* Guess what happens next.

The little girl has used her Adult, and she's done quite well considering what she's got. Unfortunately, neither mom's Parent (who knows what *should* be worn to parties) nor her Child (who is afraid the other kids and their mothers will laugh at Sally Sue and herself) likes the result. A blast from mom's Parent blows a hole through Sally's Adult work.

"You *never* wear pajama tops with swimsuit bottoms! What could you be thinking of putting on those shoes? (etc., etc.)."

Sally, feeling naked with the top of her Adult blown off, reaches up and pulls down some Parent to cover it. She now has "clarity" that pajama tops and swimsuit bottoms clash *as a matter of fact.* It is no longer a matter of taste or opinion, but a fact.

This kind of transaction happens to us many times during those early years. Soon contaminated crazies become a "normal" and "permanent" part of our Adult.

When I was a kid, I *knew* that blue and green "clashed"; no right-minded Christian boy ever wore those colors together. This was such powerful information that I failed to oppose to it the fact that God had chosen to make his blue sky clash with his green trees. (He had used a lousy exterior decorator. He'd never have done it if he'd checked with us first.) That tape is turned down pretty low these days, partly because now "everybody's" doing it. But I still hear it from time to time,

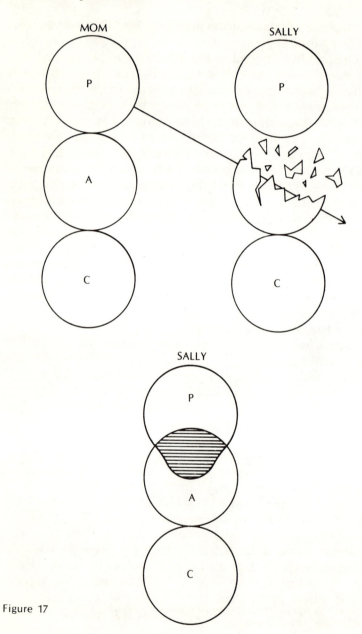

Figure 17

particularly when the colors aren't pastels. This is a case of a stubborn Parent.

The Child contaminates the Adult in a different way. The Child believes in magic.* In our early years we experience a "magic" that our Child never turns loose of. We have a gut-level conviction that certain kinds of magic work. Our Parent and Adult may tell us there is no Santa Claus, but our Child knows *there is one.* We saw the toys he brought. "Wishing *does* work," says the Child. "I wished for a pony and I got one!" (Never mind the wishes for a swimming pool; magic doesn't *always* work.) The Child feels powerful with his magic. "I said %#&$ one day, and Mommy fainted!" Years later we still believe we can make things happen by using that kind of language. Or using our anger. Or our wishing. Or our waiting.

As the Child experiences these "successes" with his magic (like "making" daddy give him a quarter by pouting), he can explain it only by overlaying his Child's belief with a piece of Adult "fact," like this:

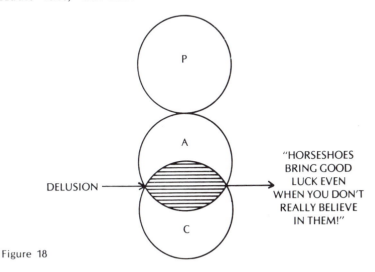

Figure 18

*You may want to read my article on magic, "If I Hold My Tongue Just Right," *Transactional Analysis Journal,* III, no. 3 (July 1973), 22-23.

The Child's contamination of the Adult is formed by early fantasies that came true.

Contamination makes ego states hard to spot. But sometimes an ego state is difficult to see for another reason: The individual has it locked up in a trunk—down in the basement. Eric Berne called this situation "exclusion."

It is possible for us to decide at some point in life (usually the early years) to exclude one or more of our ego states. The individual simply reaches out and flicks the switch to "Off." Remember the last time you were at a party and it was really fun and you switched off your Parent for the evening? Maybe you switched off your Adult, too.

Some people turn the switch to "Off" and then paste a piece of masking tape over the switch so it stays off "permanently." The decision to pretend that a part of us doesn't exist is a pathological decision and invariably leads to trouble. Can you picture the trouble you'd get into by deciding you didn't have plumbing?

The most prevalent exclusion is the Excluded Child. Many clients say to me, "I honestly don't think I have a Child!" The standard diagram for this is shown in Figure 19A. I prefer 19B (which excludes only the Little Professor and Natural Child), because I've never seen the Adapted Child excluded.

Presidents aren't supposed to show a Child ego state. When LBJ showed us his surgery scar, people got angry about it. Muskie shed a tear on television and immediately plummeted from Democratic front-runner to nowhere! The public seldom sees a politician's Natural Child. His Adapted Child is out a lot, though, and can be spotted in smiles that are apropos of nothing and in other body language that doesn't quite fit the situation.

In many ways society urges us, "Lock up your Kid." Jesus loved little children, but St. Paul (who gets listened to more than Jesus by many Christians) put down four-year-olds. He said, "When I grew up I had finished with childish things. . . . Do not be childish, my friends." Paul has successfully persuaded centuries of Christians to discount the worth of Child-

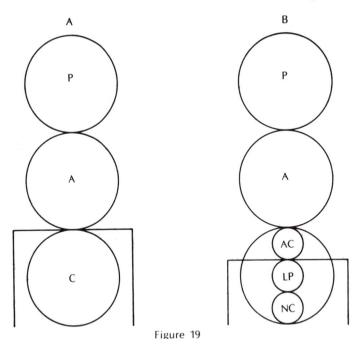

Figure 19

likeness past the age of ten. Societies still condemn "childishness." Kids bother us!

Clever little Children are a bother to Parents. Kids "goof up and goof off." They are, by some definitions, Not OK. And since most of us have a lot of Not-OK feelings in our Child ego state, we are ready to comply with what we mistakenly think the Bible tells us to do—"grow up." Add the fact that society also wants our Kid in a box.

When we voluntarily exclude our Child, we condemn ourselves to a life without real joy. "No, I'll pass up the submarine sandwiches. One piece of meat between two slices of white bread is sufficient, thank you." Life should be orderly and neat. "I had fun living once, but now I am grown up and I promise never, never to feel that joy again." (When, on occasion, we fail to keep our promise and have episodes of "feeling good," we contritely promise never to do it again.)

This is disastrous! The Child is where the hurt is. Even when he's pushed aside, he still makes the ultimate decisions that drastically influence and change our lives. If we lose touch with him, we can only wait each day to see what kind of hell he will provide.

Jesus spoke of "the sin against the Holy Spirit." This came when folk asked him if there was an unforgivable sin. He said there was only one, refusing to acknowledge we are forgivable! Or denying there is someone who could cure us. The cure always involves our Child. Emotional pain arises when we "sin against the Child." When we willfully and consciously separate ourselves in a hundred different ways from our Child ego state, the Kid will handle it in his own way, and usually it hurts!

Locked up in the cellar, the Child resorts to guerrilla warfare, but this isn't our worst loss. The saddest part is that we are deprived of all the goodies only the Child can experience.

Occasionally I have seen something that looks like the Excluded Child but isn't. Some Children are simply "square":

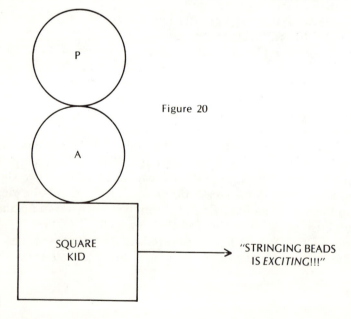

Figure 20

This individual has a Child, all right; it just doesn't "swing" by popular standards. He gets turned on by counting the fly spots on the ceiling. The biggie of his day is listening to paint dry. I'm not putting this down, that is, my *Adult* isn't putting it down, but I admit that my Child is giggling at how square that dumb kid is. Yet who am I to decide what "fun" is for someone else?

A woman confessed to me that the thing that would excite her most would be to join a literary society. Since neither my Parent nor my Child digs literary societies, I was tempted to "help" her by pointing out how very dull this could be. But she has a perfect right to enjoy what she will, so I kept my mouth shut and helped her to fulfill her wish.

The Child, as I said, is the most commonly excluded ego state, but some people decide to exclude both their Parent and their Adult. These folk are real freaks. Without a Parent to nurture or provide guidelines, and without an Adult to stay in touch with reality, they simply groove on whatever their Child wants at any given moment. An alcoholic decommissions his

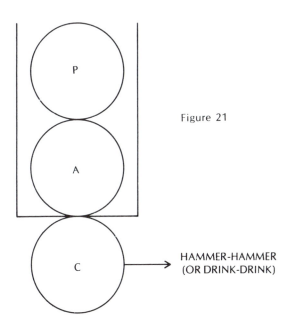

Figure 21

HAMMER-HAMMER
(OR DRINK-DRINK)

Parent and Adult. He's like a "hammer freak." A hammer freak loves to pound nails into boards. He doesn't care about eating or things like that. He just digs hammering.

Religious freaks get their jollies by standing around saying (or shouting) "religious" words. There was this guy who stood on campus yelling, "Jesus, Lord!" Nobody else could study, but they wouldn't get back at him because he was doing it for Jesus! You can inform a religious freak that someone has just cut off three of his toes, and he'll answer, "God is great and God is good." He has his Child turned up so loud that reality never bothers him.

Little Children need some supervision. I suppose that's why God gave us two other ego states. Hammer freaks usually wind up nailing their feet to the floor. Winos freeze to death. Glue sniffers turn their brains to putty. Thank God for Parents and Adults!

Middle-class males are especially susceptible to another double exclusion. An individual discovers he gets paid for

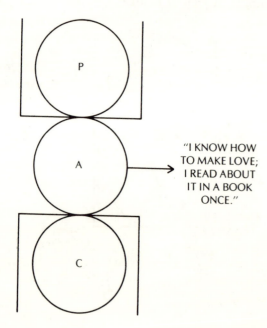

"I KNOW HOW TO MAKE LOVE; I READ ABOUT IT IN A BOOK ONCE."

Figure 22

having a superproficient Adult, so he decides to spend the rest of his life in that ego state.

He spends very little time nurturing himself or others. He "has fun"—in the manner of an adding machine. He carefully chooses a wife who will look after all the Parent/Kiddy stuff at home. If a crisis breaks out, he analyzes, sorts, and postulates. He pretends he's a senior executive with a logistical problem. His wife hates his endless "staff studies." Fun for him is two martinis after work—no more, no less, and always with a precise amount of vermouth. Fun is someone bringing up the fuel shortage at dinner so he can explain how oil-depletion allowances work. He invariably leaves home at 8:03 AM, carrying his attache case on the left side. He fills his days with factual facts and decisive decisions.

Behold the Complete Adult on Saturday. He watches the Oilers play what they call football. He enjoys it only if the announcer provides him with 39,000 statistics, for how else would a computer enjoy football?

"Wow, sports fans! This is a new record in the number of times a defensive left tackle has pulled up his pants in the end zone during the first half!" Where do they get all those statistics?

It isn't entertainment if it doesn't go through his computer. His father's favorite motto was, "Think hard enough and you'll get it right!" It's when the TV blows a tube that the Complete Adult finds himself in heaven. Now he gets to pore over the schematic diagram and consult the *Encyclopedia Britannica.*

I've said it before and I'll say it again, *living* in the Adult is not—repeat *not*—what TA or the gospel advocates. To me, it's living death.

The slowly dying "Dogma for Women of the Middle Class" has produced another exclusion, the Excluded Adult. Some girls learn early that if they want to catch a male, they mustn't look too bright. They exclude their Adult except when it serves the Parent function.

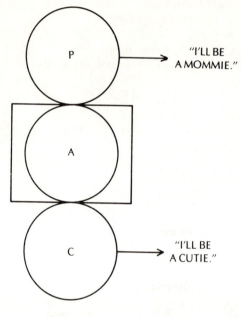

Figure 23

This girl spends her time nurturing, criticizing, playing, whining, and laughing. She permits herself to know where to put the soap in the washing machine only because it helps her be a "better mother." She can drive the car but has "no idea what that funny jiggly thing up front" is. She can add a twenty-seven-inch-long grocery tape at a glance but gets "so confused" with bank statements. (She has kept her 3.6 average in college a deep, dark secret!)

A lady with this particular exclusion usually marries Mr. Computer (above), and between them they have a whole person.

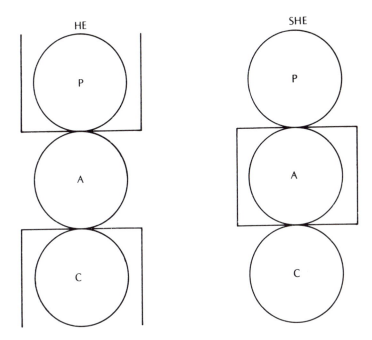

Figure 24

This relationship looks like a "marriage." Unfortunately, three other ego states are going to waste and causing trouble. The irony is that between them they could be *two* whole persons!

Exclusion can be an important concept for analyzing church groups and other organizations. In some churches members leave their Adult behind when they enter the sanctuary. For them, religion is never rational. I remember hearing of a college professor, a geologist, who spent his weekdays teaching kids to recognize rocks created "billions of years ago." But on Sundays, when he taught Bible history, he adamantly asserted that the world was created in 4004 B.C., "like the Bible teaches." At the time, I wondered how he could do that. Now I understand. His Parent came to church while his Adult stayed home and read the funnies to his Child.

Other churches throw the Kid out as well. Their worship and social experiences are "For Parents Only." They "point with pride" and "view with alarm." They play religious versions of "Ain't It Awful?"

Some denominations post a sign out front reading ADULTS ONLY. They discuss things. They love to "hear both sides of an issue." (That makes some sense to me, but I notice they never invite a madam in to tell her side of the story.) Whatever they do is rated X. Adults only.

Many churches cater only to Kids. They sing rollicking "gospel hymns" as all five-year-olds do. "Sing them over *again* to me, Wunnerful words of Lye-yif." They avoid Gregorian chants and anything written by Bach. If the hymn can be accompanied by a rinky-tink piano, so much the better. The Kids love it. Then the Parent-in-the-Pulpit uses scripture to beat the hell (pun intended) out of his Child-only crowd. And strangely, they love that too. They have a secret agreement: He will only attack them collectively, never as individuals. Father-Daddy tells his Children-Who-Want-To-Adapt what they're doing wrong, what they mustoughtshould do, and how many pretties he and God will give if they ever shape up. They also have a secret agreement that they never will shape up, because if everyone shaped up they would have to figure out a whole new operation. A pastor of one of these churches quips, "Of course I like sin. Without sin I'd be out of a job, ha, ha!" He isn't kidding.

Some churches are meaningful to all three ego states. I've been to quite a few that hooked "all three" of me. Some very useful and helpful Parent tapes were reinforced; I received new information and new insights into my life; and my Child was nurtured and stroked. All this was accomplished without the church relying on the "authority" of Nashville or Rome. TA people call that a bull's-eye! The church had hit all *three* targets.

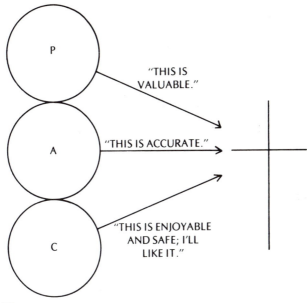

Figure 25

7

Who's Saying What to Whom?

A good way for Sammy and Sally to stay in trouble is for them to assume that only two people are present when they're talking to each other. There are at least six people involved in any "two-way" conversation. Listen:

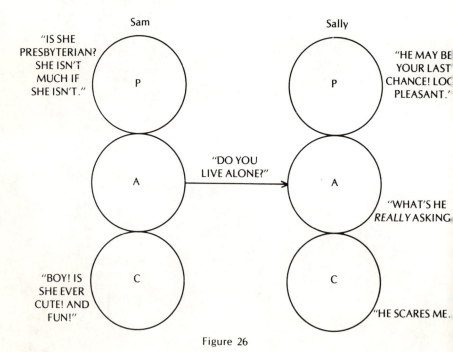

Figure 26

In this chapter, we'll look at dialogues between ego states. Some dialogues occur between individuals; others occur inside an individual's head.

Let's look at the "insiders" first. When you're driving down the freeway, you think a lot, right? You tackle a problem and you "think it through." By the time you arrive at your destination, you are thoroughly confused. And because your Adapted Child is willing to take the blame for anything, you're persuaded you're dumb.

(There's a great World War II story that illustrates "I'll-take-the-blame" behavior. In France the American army hurled a volley of shells into a small village and then occupied it. In the rubble of a house soldiers find a dazed *grand-pere* sitting nude in the bathtub, the stopper dangling from his hand. Over and over he mumbles, "All I did was pull out the plug!")

One person may think consistently (note I said *may*), but we are *not* one person. Man, created in the image of his God, is three persons, but not always a "blessed" trinity.

Using our basic diagram, there are six ways that "who" can talk to "whom" in our heads.

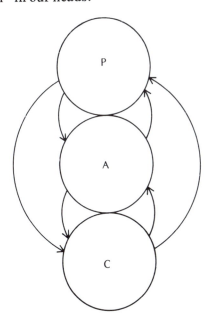

Figure 27

When we add the possible ways that other ego states can respond, we then have a total of twelve combinations. We call each combination (the verbal stimulus and its response) a "transaction."

The manner in which you keep yourself company can either be helpful or mess you up. Since your head belongs to you, you get to choose how you want it to work. Since your head belongs to you, you get to choose how you want it to work. Since your head belongs to you, you get to choose how you want it to work. (Don't blame the typesetter; I decided to write this down twice because it's an important idea, and a *new* one for a lot of folk.)

One internal transaction seems universal. The Parent beats on the Child.

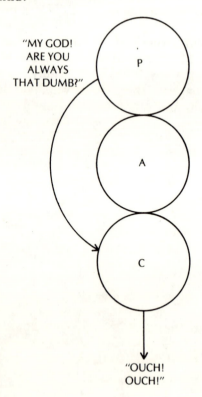

Figure 28

Fritz Perls called this the self-torture game. Some people discover early that they can get attention (if only if their own head) by scolding themselves. They decide to smoke, whereupon they beat on themselves for smoking and then explain why they "can't quit." Then they beat on themselves for being spineless. And on and on.

Beating on ourselves or other persons as a "way to abundant life" has often attracted theological and religious support. The world's history is full of hair-shirt wearing, scapegoating, breast-beating, and virgin sacrifice.

In my experience, few churches have faced up to, and acknowledged, the constant Kicking Syndrome. We have theologized our way into maintaining our belief that people grow best when they are hit a lick. No matter how subtly the contract is worded, many congregations hire pastors to play Critical Parent to their Adapted Children. He is to urge, cajole, plead, criticize, nag, beg, and press—all in a "nurturing and fatherly way." Many pastors wear collars, stoles, hoods, and robes in the hope that these will help them stand taller and accomplish this impossible task. (I know that's why *I* wore them for a long time! And many of my brothers "of the cloth" have admitted the same.) This sets up the Game: Depending upon the track record of that particular congregation, the pastor will in time find himself responsible for every act and emotion in his parish, and either people will say, "Gee, you're wonderful, Father Murgatroyd," or the roles will switch and the outraged congregational Parent will scold the pastoral Child-who-tried-but-failed and ask him to find another field of wider service.

I sees self-flagellation in some acts that the church calls "confession of sin." Confession *could* be a really neat Adult operation. Confession is a chance to re-evaluate where we are and what's getting in our way. Knowing that, we can take effective action. But most confessions of sin are done from the Adapted Child position and result in bad feelings. "I'm no good; I failed again. Even God must go 'Yukkk' when he sees *me* coming" (beat, beat, beat). Then the pastor, in the name of the Nurturing-Parent-in-the-Sky, signifies that we will be forgiven, *not* because we're worth a damn, but because we felt bad enough.

Biblical theology believes God forgives people while they are sinning, but earthly Parent ego states don't buy that; consequently, the potentially helpful confession often is turned into an orgy of self-recrimination. This, in turn, reinforces the conviction that there is no hope for us. We'll just have to "try harder"—and fail again.

One of my favorite folk heroines was lying on what she assumed to be her deathbed. She took communion but absolutely refused to say the confession from the Book of Common Prayer. Her contention was that she had never been a worm and a wretch, never intended to be, and wasn't about to insult God by claiming that he had goofed in his creation.

Who gets to hold forth in *your* head? You might want to loosen up the protocol. Since it's your head, you can learn ways to allow whichever ego states you like to get a word in edgewise when familiar patterns begin unfolding. This is a must for people who want to change and get rid of the pain and hurt of their loused-up lives. There is no way whatsoever for a person to find abundant life while beating the hell out of himself.

We've been brainwashed. Beating isn't any way to correct ourselves. Correction is the job of the Adult ego state, and Adults never scold, they merely report. The Adult can give us the information we need without a lot of passionate garbage getting in our way.

When I encounter a proficient self-beater, I ask him to attempt to stand up while using one leg to kick the other leg off the floor. Invariably he'll wail, "How can I?" Then he gets the point. You can't stand up while you're beating yourself down. No one ever got well of anything by being scolded. This is true inside our heads, too. Parent-to-Child scoldings serve only one purpose. They invite the Child to "feel bad," and the Child usually succumbs.

Parental scolding produces depression in the Child. One

night, eager to finish *Future Shock,* I went to bed and got comfy. The section I read described thirty-three-year-old Ph.D.'s receiving federal grants of several million dollars with which they were doing great, exciting things. I was grooving on this good stuff, but suddenly a wave of depression rolled over me.

There was nothing depressing in the things I was reading, so the red flag in the back of my head (which waves when something goes haywire) went up. The first procedure I use for exploring depression is to find out what the Parent is laying on the Child. I sat there quietly and listened. It didn't take long to hear the voice of my Parent: "You slob! How come you ain't got a doctorate? How come you ain't getting lots of money from the government to do big important things for the world? These kids are doing it, and you're forty-five years old! We didn't send you to college so you could be a nobody! They don't even know who you are in the next state, much less Washington. Blah, blah, blah."

Man! No wonder I was feeling depressed. When I got in touch with my "crazies," some options opened. I turned off my Critical Parent, who wasn't making any sense at all, and turned on my Nurturing Parent, who gave me some good strokes. My Adult reviewed all the things I *have* done with my life, and in a while the depression eased. But remember, bad feelings don't go away instantly. It takes a minute or two for the chemicals in the brain to cool down once they've been heated.

Try an experiment. Pick something you think you can get mad about. Now think about it, hard! Work at it for a minute. Get even madder! Notice how you can do it? Actors use the same technique to project great emotion. It's called "method acting." They really feel the emotion they are trying to show.

If you can make yourself feel something, it follows that you can also *stop* yourself from feeling it. People who say they can't quit feeling a certain way usually are getting a reward, however distorted, out of feeling that way. More about this later.

There is a feeling similar to "depression" called "despair," and it occurs when the Child listens in on a conversation between the Adult and the world of reality and doesn't like what he hears. For example, my wife informs me she's having an affair with the butcher to solve the high cost of groceries. This is Adult information the Child doesn't want to hear. The Child experiences despair. (Theologians call this "existential" despair. It preaches good.)

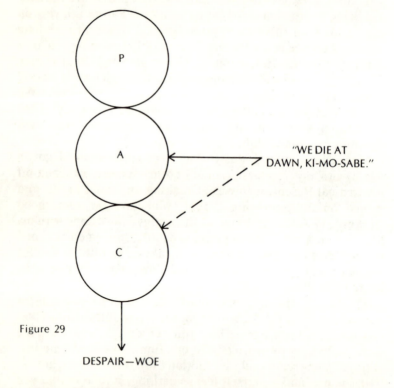

"WE DIE AT DAWN, KI-MO-SABE."

Figure 29

DESPAIR — WOE

Kids don't like to hear the bad news of death, sickness, doing without, and the like. We feel sunk. But despair is a natural function of life, and in time we recover.(Exceptions include the event diagramed in Figure 29.)

Often our Critical Parent makes hay while the sun is extinguished. Most of us learn to beat on ourselves (or someone else) in order to avoid feeling despair or coping with it. The Critical Parent begins its familiar chant, "This wouldn't have happened if you had done so-and-so." Now the Child in us has two things to deal with: the onslaught of despair *plus* the depression caused by the Parent. Having to work through your wife's new relationship with the butcher is tough enough, but trying to deal with that while your Parent "reminds" you that it wouldn't have happened if you hadn't quit jogging and lost your shape is as difficult as it would be for a one-armed man with hives to hang wallpaper.

When we understand what's going on inside us, we can function more adequately outside. And to understand what's happening inside us doesn't require an expert with four college degrees; he can't see inside your head anyway. You are the best expert on what's going on in there—*if you start listening.* Unfortunately, we have repeatedly been told that paying attention to ourselves is un-Christian and selfish. We ignore ourselves until it gets to be a habit. It's more useful to pay attention to how we operate and to make effective changes than it is to wait until we explode. Sooner or later you *will* pay attention to yourself. The longer you wait, the worse the results.

Sammy and Billy Bob stand on a street corner and talk. Looks like a simple affair, but now you understand that it's quite a convention. Each has a lot of voices going on inside his head: "Hope he likes me." "Stand up straight so he'll be impressed." "Where will we eat?" "What was it Martha wanted me to get at the store?" "What is he trying to get me to hear?"

As Sammy speaks to Billy Bob, a minimum of three people listen. Each of Billy Bob's listening ego states hears Sammy from a specialized point of view. Moreover, each has his own response patterns. This makes for a lot of options.

When Sammy decides to speak to Billy Bob, he has *nine*

possible ways of speaking. Each of his three ego states can talk to any of Billy Bob's three ego states.

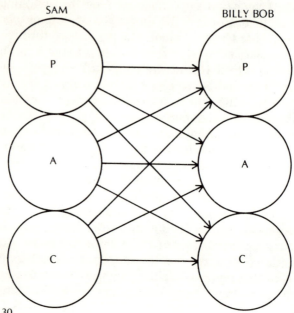

Figure 30

Having noticed a girl in a see-through blouse, Sam wants to comment on the way kids dress nowadays. He has a minimum of nine options.

PARENT TO PARENT: These girls are just asking to be raped!

PARENT TO ADULT: I wouldn't allow a daughter of mine to dress that way!

PARENT TO CHILD: Quit ogling her.

ADULT TO PARENT: Would you be angry if your daughter dressed that way?

ADULT TO ADULT: Do you think underwear is on its way out?
ADULT TO CHILD: Does that excite you, or make you nervous?
CHILD TO PARENT: What girl? I didn't even look!
CHILD TO ADULT: Want to know what I'm feeling?
CHILD TO CHILD: (Expletive deleted.)

To each of these statements Billy Bob has nine possible responses. For each transaction between these two people, given the three main ego states, there are (9 x 9 = 81) eighty-one possible ways to go! Unfortunately, we spend most of our lives relying on the same one or two transactions we learned at our mother's knee (and at other joints).

If we insist on relating to people in only one or two ways, we're really in a rut (a grave with the ends knocked out). Learning to use all our ego states in a conscious way gives us options, and options are critical. The fewer options you have, the more anxiety you will experience. If you decided years ago to get angry (or hurt) whenever someone insults you, you also decided in that moment to stay tense most of your life. Every time someone opens his mouth, you must be ready to do an anger or a hurt. With every conversation a potential problem, life gets tense.

You can explore other options. I frequently ask people to invent multiple responses to a given remark, one from each facet of their personalities. They come up with some dandies. Folk with freed-up Little Professors invent happy responses.

Yesterday my son plotched down at the table while I was typing and began talking with his mouth full. I was crabby at the interruption *and* at not being able to understand him. Without thinking I sent my Critical Parent out to scold him: "All I heard was 'Mrmph grppst brttlt.' " His response came from his Little Professor, "That was pret-ty *close,* Dad!" I broke up in laughter. My grumpies were gone, and he was pleased with himself.

We usually stay with old, ineffective options because the

Parent-in-our-head insists that's the only way to go. "Honesty is the best policy *always,* right?" It may be the best policy, but it isn't *always* useful. Being accurate isn't always useful either, no matter how often my Parent says so. Telling another person, "When I see you coming I get sick to my stomach," may be both honest and accurate, but it isn't useful unless I really never ever want to see him again.

The Pharisees were so involved with being "honest and accurate" with the law that they failed to understand its spirit. Jesus saw them "straining out gnats and swallowing camels." Why tell your husband his tie is in the soup if you know he never uses that sort of information? Or if it always leads to a fight?

If our old tried-and-true options aren't working, it's time to try some new ones.

Transactions between two people can take one of three forms. Being familiar with each form and knowing how to use or avoid it increases our options.

Complementary transactions are simply conversations between any *one* of my ego states and any *one* of yours. So long as we each remain in that same state, the conversation can go on forever. This can be either pleasant or horrendous, depending on the situation.

> CHILD TO CHILD: C1: Let's goof off.
> C2: Sure. Whattaya wanna do?
> C1: Let's go watch the stock market.
> C2: Can I peek at the secretaries?
> ADULT TO ADULT: A1: What time is it?
> A2: Three o'clock.
> A1: Do you think we have time to finish our work?
> PARENT TO CHILD: P: You should be ashamed of yourself, Mr. Jones!
> C: I know. Sometimes I just don't understand why I act this way.

If we want the conversation to continue, it is important that we both remain in the ego state we started with. If one of us switches to another ego state, the transaction is *crossed*.

> HUSBAND (ADULT TO ADULT):   We have another flat tire.
> WIFE (CHILD TO PARENT):   Why do you expect me to be responsible for the car?

The missus, by responding to thoughts in her head instead of his words, has crossed the transaction. They're no longer talking about tires, but about his expectations of her. This kills the dialogue unless he perseveres.

Crossed transactions can be useful on occasion, as when the conversation needs to be stopped:

> PARENT TO CHILD: That's a horrible-looking shirt you're wearing!
> ADULT TO ADULT: Do you really want me to feel bad?

The arrows don't have to cross to produce a crossed transaction:

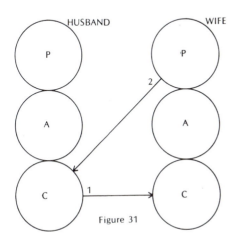

Figure 31

HUSBAND (*after his second martini*): Let's go hide from the kids (*hint, hint*).

WIFE (*after a hard day—and now this*): Go put the plates on the table and act your age.

Ulterior transactions, the third form of transactions, are the sneaky ones. These are the crooked, gamy, and psychologically freighted messages that say two different things simultaneously. One message is "straight," but the tone of voice or a key word sends a second message to be understood "psychologically."

Ulterior transactions come in two forms. One is angular: The arrows of the dual transaction literally form an angle. (The speaker has an angle too!)

In a modulated voice Reverend Bodelschwing says, "You weren't in church Sunday, Sam. Was anything wrong?" He

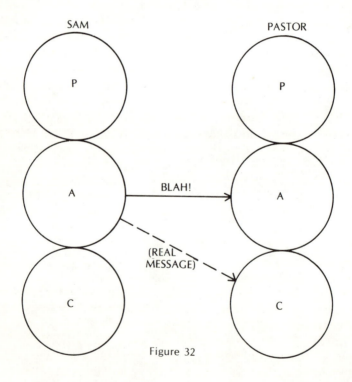

Figure 32

knows danged well nothing was wrong. Sam went fishing. The question is ostensibly Adult to Adult, but the preacher's eyes betray the psychological "hook" that is dangling for Sam's Child to grab. The "furtive message" is clear: "Remember, Sam, we want church to come before fishing."

The course of the dialogue depends on which message Sam responds to. Sam can say (Adult to Adult), "No, nothing was wrong." Or (Child to Parent), "Gee, I'm sorry. I'll try to make it next week."

The other kind of sneaky transaction is two-leveled and is called a *duplex* transaction. Again two separate messages are sent out, as in angular transactions. But whereas in the angular transaction the Adult is *deliberately* trying to hook the other person's Child, in the duplex transaction the message-sender has two ego states wanting to talk at the same time.

George wants a shirt to put on. His Parent is also upset because his wife didn't do the laundry "like she was supposed to." He kills two birds with one stone (or so he thinks) by asking, "Sally, dearest, where did you hide my shirt *this* time?" He wants to know (Adult to Adult) where his shirt is *and* he coats that request for information with a not-so-clever scold.

Or, George asks his wife, "What time do the kids get home from school?" Adult. But the twinkle in his eye and lilt in his voice are from his Child. Now, George's and his wife's Adults *can* discuss bus schedules—or their Kids can plan some fun. Which of George's two messages will she answer? If she has a grudge, she may tell him the children get home in ten minutes, then go off to make cheese blintzes.

We have trained ourselves to use sneaky transactions whenever possible. We say one thing, mean another. The other person is expected to "fill in the blanks."

Bill Gentry, a TA therapist and my good friend, uses this term in an exercise for looking at marriage transactions. The partners frequently like to play "Can You Guess as Good as I Can?" When Sam says, "I'm thirsty . . ." Sally is expected to fill in the blank, in this case, ". . . and I'd like it if you brought me a Coke. Will you?"

Filling in the blanks is a good way to get into trouble if the second person guesses incorrectly. Ulterior transactions require the listener to guess which of several possible messages is the real one, as in a multiple-choice exam. Mrs. Fangschleister says to her husband, "We don't go out much anymore." Mr. F.'s Little Professor knows there's a second message in there somewhere, and he's supposed to figure it out. But which message to choose?

(a) You're getting old, fat, and lazy.

(b) Ask me to go somewhere.

(c) I wouldn't be seen in public with you, but I would still like to be asked.

(d) None of the above. Don't bother to respond; I just wanted to hit you a lick and watch you worry.

If Mrs. F. chose to turn this into a straight transaction, she would tell her husband what she felt and what she wanted him to do. "I would really like to see the opera with you. Will you buy us tickets for Friday?" No guessing involved.

While we're discussing transactions, I'd like to share one more with you. It's not "official," but it's a good one to notice. It's variously tagged "diluted," "ricochet," and "gossip." This transaction is bounced off a third person.

Dad looks at Sammy's new suit. He turns to Mom and says, "Sammy looks nice in his new suit." Mind you, Sammy himself is standing right there! He may get some "enjoys," but it's like drinking milk wrung out of a dishrag. In TA groups we insist that people speak *to* people instead of speaking *about* them. If Sam has a goodie coming, why not give it to him directly instead of bouncing it around the room? Sam can wonder, "How come Dad won't tell *me* I look nice?"

Some therapists encourage "ricochets" on the theory that

indirect transactions help people to slowly become familiar with one another. I disagree. They can learn right off that they won't turn into a pillar of salt if they speak directly to another person.

Some church people encourage indirect transactions for the same reason. In the parish, "before TA," I spent a lot of time carrying messages between the interested individuals. I also wondered why I was "in the middle" so much—and in hot water so much. "Reverend, you've got to tell the organist to quit playing the hymns so slowly!" Now I understand that I don't "got to," and would encourage people to relate to each other directly—as real people.

8

The Land of the
Warm Fuzzies

One of the major problems for "schools" of psychology has
been, "What makes people tick?" Eric Berne thought the
great question of existence was why people bother to talk to
one another. At first this sounded silly to me, but it became a
really heavy question when I thought about it. Why indeed?
Why do you bother to do the things you do? We are all
motivated by something.

People want to know, "How can I motivate So-and-so?" I
don't have an answer, because the *question* isn't valid.
Everyone is already motivated. Often what a father is really
saying (not *asking*) is, "I don't *like* my son's brand of
motivation. He's motivated to lie around all day and stare at
the ceiling." Dad wants his son to be motivated to do what
dad wants him to do.

TA has come up with a clearer idea of what the motivating
"something" is. The answer came out of a medical discovery.
A physician, Rene A. Spitz, attempted to determine why
certain newborns become seriously ill (and many of them die)
for no apparent reason. (The hospital charts carry the entry,
"Failure to thrive.") Spitz found one common factor: an
absence of fondling. Medical science now knows that human
beings have a physical need to be touched, especially during
the first few weeks of their lives. And they usually get it,

because people *like* to hold babies. Mothers hold them for feedings; they bathe and rub their bodies. But some infants don't get enough fondling, and these may develop the disease called marasmus.

TA maintains that later on the physical need for fondling is replaced to some degree by a physical need for recognition and attention. TAers says, "If you don't stroke me, my back will curl and I'll die!"

TA believes your Child ego state has a *physical* need to be "stroked," either physically or verbally. Dr. Harold Russell of the University of Texas Medical Branch in Galveston has demonstrated that people respond physically to verbal stroking. He hitched me up to instruments for measuring skin temperature. Then he said, "I'm sure glad you've come to see me." I was not aware of any physical or emotional change, yet his instruments recorded an increase in skin temperature of two degrees in five seconds flat.

Strokes are as essential as food, air, water, or sleep. You can't do without them and stay healthy. TA theory declares that we are motivated by our need for attention and strokes. We do everything with one eye on the number of strokes we'll get.

Lots of people experience stroke deprivation. At a party the hosts' young son toddles in and begins beating on the coffee table with a block. The parents (because they've read a lot of "good" books) ask their guests to ignore him. "He just wants attention." If our theory holds water, this is as cruel as it would be to ignore a kid with skinny arms and legs and a bloated belly crawling across the floor and reaching up for some potato chips. Slapping his son's hand away, dad announces to his guests, "Don't pay any attention to him; he just wants food." Not giving attention to people who are starving for attention is as funny as a rubber crutch.

The Zulus must have known about stroking. When a child was born, he was guaranteed a full two years of naked-body contact. At all times he was either at his mother's bare breast or strapped to her nude back. If she bore another child during those two years, the older child was transferred to a foster mother and the physical contact maintained. Then, at age two, he joined his waiting brothers and sisters, who, having been well stroked in their own infancy, were happy to receive him and love and nurture him. The result? Little juvenile delinquency and few problem children.

The white man decided the Zulus needed to be "civilized." Fathers were carted off to work in the big city, leaving mothers to carry the home workload and do all the parenting single-handedly, and so the two years of "freeloading" ended. The result of this "progress" has been skyrocketing delinquency and much social unrest. Stroking is a critical requirement!

We can be stroked in two ways: positively or negatively. This is sometimes called "positive and negative reinforcement." My Parent is pleased that I know such big words and my Adult can handle them, but my Kid doesn't understand such terms. He prefers the term introduced by TA pioneer Dr. Claude Steiner, who called a positive stroke a warm fuzzy.*

A warm fuzzy is having your daughter crawl up in your lap and declare, "If I could choose from all the daddies in the world, I'd still pick you." Wow! Your skin literally feels warm and fuzzy all over. Another warm fuzzy: walking into a party where you know nobody and seeing a face across the room suddenly brighten and smile at you. It's having your back rubbed, your hand held; it's being paid a compliment. Whereas a stroke is anything that says in any way, "I see you!" a warm fuzzy is someone recognizing you in a *pleasant* way.

The opposite sort of stokes—the *un*pleasant ones—Steiner called cold pricklies. You feel cold and prickly all over. A cold

---

*Dr. Steiner, author of *Games Alcoholics Play, Scripts People Write,* and numerous major contributions to the *Transactional Analysis Journal,* is one of the TA leaders who are much concerned with using our skills to correct social, as well as individual problems.

prickly is being told, "You don't sweat much *for a fat boy.*" It's walking into a room and seeing someone turn away. It's having your hand slapped, being scolded, or being sworn at. You don't like it; it makes for problems. Even so, by everything that's holy, it's still a stroke!

Back in my freshman year in college, a grown-up sophomore I respected said, "I'd rather be hated than ignored," and I thought he was wondrous wise. Rollo May is widely quoted today saying the same thing: "The opposite of love is not hate. The opposite of love is indifference." We cannot tolerate a *no*-stroke situation.

Picture walking down the street and meeting an acquaintance. You say, "Good morning" (a stroke, an "I see you"), and he passes by without giving you so much as a glance. What do you experience in your gut? I ask this a lot when I lecture. People say they feel like throwing something at the nonresponder, tackling him, screaming at him. When we fail to get an expected fuzzy, our reaction is physical.

I remember coming home one evening after work and cheerily greeting my family with, "I'm home, team!" No answer. Barbara had the phone stuck in her ear, Dan had his clarinet stuck in his mouth, and Julie had her face stuck in a television set. I tried again and still no answer. Instead of trying a third time, I walked over to a mirror and checked to make sure I was really there. (In childhood I had a horrible fantasy of being turned invisible and inaudible. No matter how loudly I yelled, nobody could see or hear me. I avoided this situation in real life by becoming a preacher.)

Because we can't stand no-stroke situations, it's important in TA to examine individual and family "stroke economies." How does one set up his life to get the strokes he needs? We believe people manage their lives to gain the maximum number of "I see you's."

If, as you read this, you hear noises in your head saying you shouldn't need attention, stop and consider this: You wouldn't listen if the voice were telling you it's "wrong" to worry about getting enough air, would you? Strokes are as necessary as air!

Getting strokes would all be attended to rather straightforwardly of it weren't for society's needs. Down through the years each society has developed a *managed* stroke economy. Men know intuitively that this vital need for strokes can be used to control people, whether as a nation, a family, or as individuals.

Sam and Sally get married and settle down. Then comes Sam Junior. Very unsettling. For a while he's fun, but soon he's turning life into terror. How to teach him to quit "watering his garden" in the middle of the new rug? How to make him stop pulling the drapes off the rod? The cat is on strike until Sammy will quit pouring molasses in her ear. Because society is concerned more with how people perform than how they feel, the most effective way to control Sammy seems to be with a managed stroke economy based on performance. Control his warm fuzzies. When Sammy "misbehaves," withhold them. He catches on quickly. To get a fuzzy, he has to "do right" and "be a good boy."

The result is trouble. Most people are stroke-starved. And stroke-starved folk develop their own stroke economy—similar to our dollar economy in which dollars are so dear and powerful that we guard them with our lives. We figure we have only a limited supply of fuzzies, and when they're gone, there'll be no more.

The Great Depression came about mainly because there was a shortage of dollars (and francs, lira, pounds, etc.). People jumped from high buildings; they starved; they turned to crime—all because of a shortage of symbols of wealth. In 1929 people needed the same things they had needed previously—food, clothes, transportation, pleasure, homes—but these things became unavailable because the symbols of wealth weren't available. It took a dozen years and a major war to rescue us from our insanity. Barry Stevens uses the same example in *Don't Push the River*.

Our managed stroke economy is insane. Impressions to the contrary, there is no shortage of warm fuzzies. I once asked a man who refused to stroke others to lie to himself and pretend he liked it. He was to go around the room and stroke people indiscriminately. He stroked a lot of people—awkwardly at first, but with increasing zeal. Afterward he said, "Wow! I really feel great!" He also felt "fuller." And, miracle of miracles, he had more strokes in his stroke bank than before his spending spree.

The Protestant Work Ethic is a social myth that prevents us from receiving the strokes we need. "I will only accept a stroke if I deserve it, and my Parent gets to decide when that is." I once congratulated a man for a neat piece of work. Instead of saying thank you (the only adequate answer to a warm fuzzy), he replied, "Oh, it just came to me. I didn't do anything." This guy wasn't allowed to take a stroke unless he was covered with sweat.

People duck strokes if their Parent disapproves of their accepting.

A: I like your hairdo.
B: I washed my hair and I can't do a thing with it.

A: You look sexy today.
B: I'm really tired.

A: What a neat tie you have on.
B: It's my brother's.

Obeying Parental orders to duck a stroke allows a degree of "defensiveness": "You can't reach me, even with a goodie!" It's also an act of hostility. When you say something nice to me and I reject it as untrue or undeserved, I am slyly saying, "You ass! You wouldn't recognize a nice hairdo if you saw one." In any event, we continue to avoid what we desperately need.

Another way to duck a stroke is to play Stroke Ping-Pong.

A: I like your dress.
B: Your necklace is charming, too.

This sounds like each person is receiving a stroke, but I don't think so. B is "not allowed" to receive the first stroke, so she pings it back.

Some of us can accept strokes only when they are socially correct. In a letter to the editor of the University of Houston's *Daily Cougar,* a coed complained that as she was passing a bunch of boorish young men working on a new building, she was assaulted by loud comments on her protuberances. Her references to Male Chauvinist Piggism testified to her sense of outrage.

While not justifying the conduct of these slobs, I think she missed some really neat strokes. My hunch is that she has a Parent who allows her to receive strokes only if they're extended in the "acceptable" way, meaning without sexual overtones. I also suspect she is heavily into a Game of "Proving That All Men Are Beasts," which likewise prevents stroke intake. If I could write her a happier scenario, I would have her passing the men with *outward* indifference (she would not stroke their gross behavior) while glowing inside for having been seen and admired. I'll bet this girl is pleased with her breasts, but she's awfully finicky about accepting compliments on them.

A third way to duck strokes is to evaluate them. Does the other person really mean what he says? Is the stroke truthful? How free with strokes is the giver? Again, we see strokes the way we see money—we bite the nickel to see if we want to accept it.

Houston's air is pitiful, but while I'm evaluating it, I continue breathing. I breathe it even though it's dirty, even though everyone else breathes in it, and even though I deserve better. I breathe it because I have to have air to live. I take strokes for the same reason.

Which brings me to *grace.* For thirty years I spoke of the grace of God and prayed for grace without really understanding what I was talking about. My Parent and Adult had reams of opinions and information about grace, but I never felt it until I visited New Orleans and learned about "lagniappe" (pronounced *lahn-yop*). Lagniappe is the practice of merchants giving customers "something extra," like a bottle of vanilla or a half-pound of chicory. Free, gratis. Wow! (I always say "wow" when I run into something holy, like this new insight into life.) That's exactly what grace is—something for nothing; something I haven't earned; something just given to me.

I started looking for all the "freebies" coming my way with the notion of seeing them as "grace." Double wow! Grace is everywhere. On campus a strange person sends a friendly smile (stroke/grace) my way. I drop something and someone picks it up for me (stroke/grace). My wife cooks those beloved fried potatoes. A friend apologizes for not calling but says he's thought about me a dozen times. A soft, warm wind blows across my face. Fresh water. On and on and on. Things I haven't "earned," can't justify receiving, am not "worthy of"—but am getting just the same.

One of the main messages of the Christian gospel is that God loves us. We are surrounded by grace. These free gifts of God are available to those who see them and accept them. On the other hand, the person whose Parent tape insists he must sweat to earn grace is doomed.

Put-together people, happy people, are aware of the grace in their lives. They know how to receive strokes. They realize that every good thing in their life comes to them from out of nowhere. I'm a clever, educated person and I do my share of the work, but I sure don't *earn* the love of parents, friends, loved ones, teachers, wife, children, and all the others who make it happen. Being grateful, I accept the grace that comes my way. My personal warm-fuzzy basket stays full. The abundant life can't be found when you're suffering stroke deprivation. Wanting abundant life, I am willing to stay stroked up.

Jesus observed that more will be given to the person who already "has," while the guy who "has not" will lose what little he does have. This statement is often translated into money language, and we wonder why the Lord approved something so unfair. Since Jesus' main mission was to give people life, I suspect he was talking about our inner Child. The Kid who collects all the strokes coming his way becomes a glowy, self-confident individual—which, in turn, invites more strokes. The Child who doesn't have permission to take warm fuzzies goes in another direction and invites disaster.

When we aren't allowed good strokes, we must go for bad ones—those cold pricklies. They don't feel good, but they keep our backs from curling. One of Eric Berne's most important contributions was his notion that people continue to behave poorly in order to get negative strokes for their efforts.

Since so many of our Parent tapes insist we turn away from warm fuzzies, we look elsewhere for what we need. (If you had a moral injunction against breathing, your ears would look like nostrils.) Johnny comes home with his report card. Four Bs. He gets a halfhearted "attaboy" for the Bs and some questioning why he didn't make any As. Next time he brings home three Bs and a D. The roof falls in. Dad is up out of his chair and Lecture Number 72 is playing. Mother is hovering and fanning herself. The other kids gather for the onslaught.

Johnny's Little Professor has discovered that in his family good grades are ho-hummish and expected, and if he wants strokes, Ds will do it. Next semester he brings home three Ds and an F. The cold pricklies come again. Mom and dad wonder where they went wrong. Meanwhile Johnny is being rewarded (though negatively) for being the family goof-off. From then on it's easy.

Cold pricklies keep your back from curling, and they keep you from dying, but they don't *feel* like a stroke. So your stroke basket stays feeling empty. Each cold prickly reinforces your SSI (Sorry Self-Image). You end up finding a hundred nonuseful ways of getting stroked.

Want to have fun checking this out? Pay attention to how often people come out with a "gallows laugh." A gallows laugh comes from the mouth of a guy on his way to get hanged. He turns to the crowd, smiles, and says, "Boy, is this going to teach me a lesson!" The crowd roars its approval of a man who can laugh in so sorry a plight. He gains positive strokes from the crowd, and a negative one from the noose. And dies—happy?

The heavy drinker tells his coffee klatch, "Man, did I ever fall off the wagon last night!" As he reports his failure, he smiles, and the group smiles back at him. Or, the teen-ager smilingly announces, "I always get in trouble!" Or, father announces with a grin, "I lost my job again," whereupon the family gathers around him and "comforts" him. Positive strokes for harmful behavior.

Our own Adult seldom notices the smile or laugh that accompanies our reports of woe. Our Parent says, "It would be insane to think *that* was funny." So if our attention is called to such smiles, we tend to write them off as being due to embarrassment. Actually, it's the Child who smiles. He's done it again! He knows how to get those strokes.

I can't overemphasize the importance of collecting the strokes we need. When we get enough, we've "had a good day." Consider a day when the skies are gray and lots of things go wrong, but you plow through. You feel great. You go to bed reporting you had a "wonderful, full day." Why? You got the needed strokes—of the warm fuzzy variety.

On the other hand, you've experienced days when the sun was shining and absolutely nothing went wrong, but you went to bed crabby. Why? You either didn't get the strokes you needed or your Child was sore from all the cold pricklies you collected.

At the start of a group session my cotherapist was called home because of an emergency, so I worked alone. Although I did a good job, I felt crabby afterward. I reviewed the evening and could find no cause for my crabbiness. Finally it dawned on me. With Donna absent, I had received fewer strokes—strokes the *group* doesn't provide.* She and I are

---

*Donna Wolthuis, M.S.W., is superfine with people. She "instinctively" knows where the "little Kids" are and has neat hunches about what might be useful. She's in San Antonio now. Pout.

constantly checking with each other, smiling when we notice the same thing, reinforcing each other's observations, filling in each other's omissions. With her away, I was down a hundred strokes.

Our world is full of stroke-deprived people who spend their days in "search" behavior. They search for attention. How else explain people paying hundreds of dollars to go to the West Coast and sit naked in bathtubs with other people and "learn" to rub their own derrières? They could do that at home—if they had permission. Massage parlors and houses of prostitution simply pay attention to people; prostitutes report that the attention they pay the customer is more important than the sex involved.

Taverns deliver strokes. The high priest behind the bar hears confessions and delivers sacraments. The people there accept each other's foibles. Everyone knows he's there to get stroked.

Advertisers are experts at stroking folk. "Ginger ale tastes like love." (It really tastes like *ginger ale*.) The image is, if I drink ginger ale I'll somehow get stroked. It's worth a try. "Buy a Mercadamobile and turn your neighbors green with envy." Lots of strokes in that. Remember the TV ad where a guy arrives home in his new car and every last person on the block comes running and yelling his approval and joy? For stroke-deprived people, $5,500 is cheap. You get all that attention, with a means of transportation thrown in.

Some of you are hearing your Parent ask, "Won't all that stroking give people the bighead and cause them to run berserk?" Anita Plummer says some families believe this and allow only so many warm fuzzies in a given time period. After a warm, glowy day together, father suddenly yells, for no apparent reason, "Where the hell is my magazine?" This is the signal to the family that they can quit being happy; they've just collected the last allowable fuzzy. Back to the pricklies for them. How else explain these sudden, irrational changes of mood?

No, heavily stroked people do not run berserk; it's the stroke-deprived people who run berserk. They are finding nonproductive ways of getting what they need. The ghetto woman who is always being locked up gets warm fuzzies for being the most "jail-educated" person in her cellblock. She also gets cold pricklies from the Law and from the pious. In her nonfuzzy environment, staying law-abiding means staying unstroked.*

I want to add a notion of mine. I've called it the Quest for the Superstroke: total approval of all we do, the perfect stroke in reward for the perfect performance.

Have you ever given a speech, baked a cake—whatever—and ninety-nine out of one hundred people fuzzied you to pieces but one grungy old meany held out? Used to happen to me in the pulpit. I'd preach a good sermon, and people would rave, but one grump would ask me if I was drunk when I wrote it. All afternoon I would sit and feel bad about the sermon. I had failed—no "100." Where had I gone wrong?

Mother won't feel good about her meal no matter how many compliments she receives, no matter how much food is consumed, so long as one child won't eat his spinach. We lose an awful lot of strokes if we wait for the Superstroke of Total Acceptance. It will seldom come, because there ain't none!

You may have noticed the word "permission" cropping up. This concept, another given us by Claude Steiner, is important in both TA and the Christian gospel.

People either act or refuse to act in accordance with the permission that their Parent tapes give or withhold. This is particularly obvious in how we manage to get stroked. I believe our early struggle to survive—our inculcated fear of

---

*"Ghetto woman." Translate ghetto to mean *any* tightly organized living environment, including the split-level ones. "Woman" comes from the original story—a young woman whose social worker told her, "Don't do that, you'll go to jail!" The gal smiled and did it. She had not known *how* to get to jail like all her friends.

deathly *don'ts*—is so traumatic that most of us develop a pattern of refusing to act unless we have been given specific permission.

Some people don't have permission to succeed in life. The Parent tape says, "*Nobody* in our family ever made it." "You don't have what it takes." "With a background like yours, how could you be successful?" These tapes were collected early: Mom sees her son playing tight-rope walker on the back fence. "Get down! You're going to fall!" The Kid gets the message that he isn't supposed to succeed. So he falls. Now mom gets to play "I Told You So." Mom really was *afraid* that he might fall and hurt himself, but that isn't what she said.

Other folk have permission to be "successful," but not to be *happy*. They've got scads of money and other neat things, but they're miserable. It isn't easy to be miserable in the midst of all those goodies, so they work at finding things to be miserable about. Listen for people who feel guilty about feeling good. No permission!

I've been amazed at how many graduate students don't have permission to think. Being good Adapted Children (although some are forty years old), they come to class with pencils sharpened and notebooks ready, then wait for the professor to tell them what to think. Twenty graduate students in education were asked to jot down their goals for the semester. A few minutes earlier the professor had told them that he had no expectations as to how they were to spend the year. Only two used the word "think." Most listed items like "to fulfill the requirements," "to learn what is expected of me," and "to better meet the standards of a good teacher." They didn't have permission in their heads to choose their goals.

In my work I find one lack of permission common to all people who stay in emotional pain. They don't have permission to be themselves, to feel what they feel, to think what they think. Society (both familial and civic) has asked them to perform in contrived and unchanging ways.

Change (therapy) is difficult at best; it is impossible when the individual doesn't have permission to change. Jesus understood this. His life was the enactment of the truth that *we have permission to be whole.* When Jesus played out the drama with a woman caught in adultery, he neither scolded her nor reinforced her sickness. Instead, he saw her as a real person and stroked her as a human being. He reinforced her permission to get well: "Go, and sin no more" (which roughly translates: "Lady, messing around like that isn't working out too well for you. You can change. You don't have to get rocks thrown at you unless you want to! Go find some better ways for yourself").

I want to point out that the Pharisees were getting jollies out of stoning her. People were stoned in the nude, and some of the women bounced around a lot. There is something "Freudian" about throwing stones at naked ladies. My fantasy of what went on inside the Pharisees looks something like this:

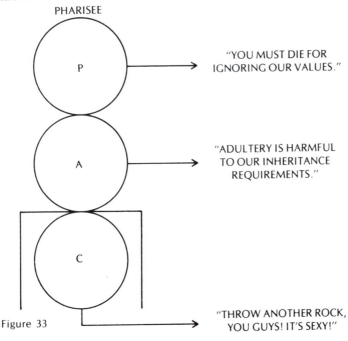

PHARISEE

P — "YOU MUST DIE FOR IGNORING OUR VALUES."

A — "ADULTERY IS HARMFUL TO OUR INHERITANCE REQUIREMENTS."

C — "THROW ANOTHER ROCK, YOU GUYS! IT'S SEXY!"

Figure 33

All three of the Pharisees' ego states were getting cared for.

Or how about the time Jesus visited the Pool of Bethsaida? Rumor was an angel would come and trouble the waters, and the first guy in would get cured. This is a spiritual form of Waiting for Santa. Jesus came upon a man who had been lying beside the pool for thirty-eight years. Jesus did a strange thing—he asked the man if he *wanted* to be healed. The man didn't answer; instead, he complained about everyone getting in his way. He avoided Jesus' directness by inviting him to play a game of "If It Weren't for Them." Jesus rejected his con with a direct act of permission: "Get up! Pack your mattress and walk!" No one had said that to the man before. Everyone assumed he *would* have gotten up if he could. But Jesus put the responsibility (that is, the ability to respond) where it belonged—with the guy with the problem. Some people are lame by choice.*

Jesus gave his followers permission to be as potent and effective as *he* was! "He who has faith in me will do what I am doing; and he will do even greater things" (John 14:12). What permission do *you* need to live a better life as you see it?

Some families give their offspring permission to be crazy; they even relish the youngster's weird ways. "This here's Sam, our crazy one. Can't do a thing with him. Do something crazy for the people, Sam! Ha, ha! There he goes again." Sam has permission to get his strokes by doing a crazy, so he *gets* them that way. He needs permission to be sane!

The concept of permission is important. Last week I watched my daughter's sixth-grade English teacher do a beautiful job of giving her student-friends permission to be creative. She laid out some of her thoughts about poem-writing, but she didn't tell them what they'd have was "poetry." That might have killed creativity. Within her helpful guidelines, each person could do almost anything and "win."

---

*This neat example of a Game preventing health is recorded in John 5:2 ff.

Julie wrote ten really neat poems. She got good grades for her creativity. I'll never have to yell at her, "Do something creative!" She already has permission.

It's hard to express creative urges when you've been trained to paint by the numbers. This only reinforces the cruddy conviction that life is to be lived "inside the lines." Lines that someone *else* drew.

For Julie, the teacher comes as "grace," a free gift. One that improves her life. Grace is everywhere when you have permission to see it, to accept it, and be grateful for it. With permission, you can live a grace-ful life!

9

You Can't Tell the Frogs
Without a Program

I don't dig opera. Some man with a stick is angry at a fat woman who sings a lot. To emphasize his anger, he shakes his stick at her; she responds by screaming back at him. I get bored.

Opera is hard for me to understand. Usually the words are sung in some foreign language. To help the audience follow the story line, a "libretto" comes with the program. The libretto is written in English. If I get dismayed at the screaming, I can stop listening and read ahead. The program lays out the entire night's work.

Transactional analysts are discovering that many people have just such a libretto for their lives. It's as if they have a drama programed into their heads, and each morning they get up, don their costumes, and go on stage and perform the next act. When the analyst and subject uncover the libretto, they can predict future life-events.

The idea that people can have a gut-level understanding of how the major events in their lives are "supposed to" unfold is spooky, yet such an understanding is frequently observed.

For example, can I have foreknowledge of when I will die? The reasonable answer is, "I have no idea," yet often the Child will have "figured it out." I asked five young women when they would die. Two said in their early forties—one by suicide, the other in an automobile accident. Another responded that she nearly died five years earlier and was living on borrowed time. (She was intent upon closing out the loan; she was drinking herself to death.) A fourth said she would die around sixty-seven of a heart attack, and the last said she would die of old age at ninety.

Let me emphasize that this isn't the Adult at work; the conclusion isn't the result of a logical process based on facts. It's the doing of the Child. During those early years the Child writes a script; then he follows it.

In writing the script the Child is influenced by three distinct sets of decisions: injunctions, traumatic decisions, and basic life position.*

In chapter 3 I discussed injunctions—those crazy messages the Adapted Child received from the Child ego state of mom and dad. (The parents *say* "Succeed!" while they act out "Please fail!") The Child concludes that "This is what mom and dad want (or don't want) me to do." The do's and don'ts become life-or-death commands. At age three we "understand" that if we disobey a don't, mother will either die or go away and let *us* die. Much later, if we haven't consciously made a new decision to replace the injunction, we still feel the injunction's power. A person with the order "Don't get too close to people" will experience physical upset on getting close.

Picture an invisible guitar string running from your mom's Child ego state to your "innards" (where we generally experience our Child). Violating an injunction feels as though someone twangs hell out of that string! (See figure next page.)

These injunctions play an important role in writing the script we chose to act out. Some injunctions, such as "Don't dislike yourself," can be helpful in life. Others, like "Don't

---

*For a more detailed discussion of life scripts, see Berne's *What Do You Say After You Say Hello?* and Steiner's *Games Alcoholics Play* and *Scripts People Live* (see Bibliography).

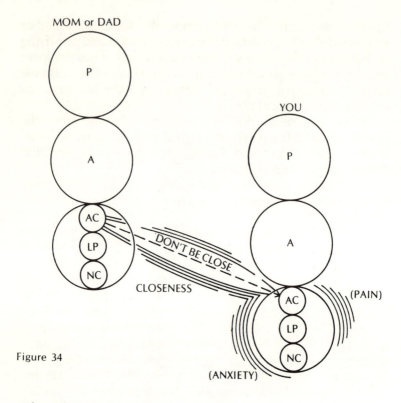

Figure 34

enjoy what you're doing," can wipe us out. For good or for evil, the Child picks a life program that insures obedience to these strongly felt orders.

Other important decisions that you made were based on "traumatic events" you experienced early in life. Let's say you were five and your dad asked how you were feeling. You felt so angry you wanted to hit him with a hammer, and you decided to share that with him. Wop, wam, blam! You ended up looking like Beetle Bailey after the Sarge got through with him. He really hurt you! For anyone that's traumatic; for a kid it's world shattering. So, not only do you decide to be more careful of what you say to dad—you decide *never* to tell *any-*

one what you're feeling. Forty years later you are still acting on that early, trauma-inspired decision. Or, you were asked to recite before company. You did and everyone laughed at you. You decided you are not a "public speaker" type, and you spend the rest of your life avoiding that situation.

These early decisions are a little guy's clever answers to big problems. Years later the answer no longer fits, but we apply it just the same. The man who still won't share his feelings—now it's his wife he shuns instead of dad—is ignoring the fact that *she* won't "destroy" him as he thought dad almost did. The guy who won't talk in public has gained communication skills since that painful boyhood experience, but he refuses to use them. Jesus spoke of three men with differing talents. The man with only one talent buried it in the ground to keep from losing it, but ended up losing it just the same. I'll bet this loser had decided—long before he had any considerable amount to handle—that he would bury any talents he received. Back there somewhere he probably caught hell for losing something and decided never to risk poor management again.

Our lives are drastically influenced not only by injunctions and traumatic events but also by a third major decision made early in life: we decided on a basic life position (BLP).* Eric Berne said all of us are born Princes or Princesses, but by the time we are five or six, society and our parents have changed us into Frogs. Although we are born Winners, most of us are soon persuaded we were destined to lose. The Frog is TA's symbol for a Loser who sits on his split-level lily pad and goes *rivvett, rivvett* for seventy years. He is waiting for someone or something to come along and kiss him and turn him back into a Prince (or turn her into a Princess).

People who have been given (or who have written for themselves) a Winner's script have adopted a BLP that says to

---

*The OK—Not OK matrix or Basic Life Position was produced by Berne and Bob Goulding, and its development is a major part of the work of Franklin Ernst, M.D.

them, "You're OK and you live in an OK world." "OK" doesn't mean great, or that nothing is wrong; it simply means acceptable. It's tough to live well if, right off, you won't accept the givens: you and your world. "OK" simply means, "I can deal with that."

The Winner (Prince) has permission to succeed, be happy, like himself, and change what he doesn't like. He knows his talents and limitations. When faced with a decision, he gets the information he needs, and then he decides. He solves his problems. Losers, however, spend their time justifying their problems. They like to explain why they're Losers.

Anytime you successfully complete a series of transactions, you are operating in the OK-OK position. For example, Sam goes to the bank to cash a check. He's OK, meaning he has money in the account and knows how to write a check. The bank is OK because it has money and check-cashing procedures. Sam may encounter obstacles ("Please write your phone number on the check"), but so long as he sees both parties as OK, the operation goes smoothly. If, on the other hand, he should decide that asking for phone numbers is "Mickey Mouse," thereby making the teller Not OK—or if the cashier decides Sam is Not OK—trouble ensues. The difficulty will continue until they get back in the OK-OK position.

Being an "OK person" doesn't mean always getting your own way. Early critics of TA saw it as creating selfish people. Not at all. The OK-OK position involves two people who respect the other person and the other person's right to have *his* needs met. Two OK people are constantly negotiating so that they *both* can have their needs met to the highest possible degree. It's not at all a matter of "You gotta do what *I* want."

Although all people move in and out of this OK-OK position in alternating fashion, only one in ten, perhaps, has adopted this as his basic *life* position. Few scripts call for Winners; most call for Frogs. If you decided long ago that you were destined to be a Frog (to spend your life waiting to live), the next step was deciding what sort of Frog to be. Frogs get to choose from among the other three basic life positions.

Before we explore this together, a warning: Loser, or Frog, does NOT mean "he never does anything right." Many who were Losers by the world's standards were Winners by their own standards—Jesus, for example. Many who were Losers by *anybody's* standards (Van Gogh?) produced much of value. Losers are not measured by production alone.

A frog can decide "I'm OK but I live in a world of Not-OK people!" This Frog spends his life "getting rid of others," one way or another. He plays "Wart" a lot. He can spot a blemish on the finest article or person. He gets what little enjoyment he's allowed by hitting people a lick. He "corners" folk to bring out the worst in them. As an Adapted Child, he takes the Socker position. He loves to take on leadership positions at church so he can talk about those "knuckleheads" who won't cooperate. "I could be an ecclesiastical Prince if it weren't for those Losers who surround me." This Frog wouldn't think of joining a church where people like each other and work together; he gives his money to a cruddy church where he can put people down.

Some Frogs decide "I'm Not OK, but the rest of the world is OK." Since Frogs are not allowed to solve their problems, they like to justify their hang-ups. "My folks bought a new toilet seat when I was six, and I never could get used to it. They ruined my Id. So what do you expect of me?" His favorite phrase is, "There I go again!" or, "I should have—why didn't I?" He picks friends who like to respond, "Because you're dumb, that's why!" He prefers to worship in a church with good leadership. "Gee, you're wonderful, Reverend Mur-gatroyd (but not wonderful enough to change *me*)." A Frog gets his jollies from turning OK people into jelly.

A psychiatrist-friend had a patient who smoked, drank coffee, chewed gum, and ate mints—all at the same time—during therapy. The patient was what you could call a very oral person. Since my friend was the twelfth consecutive psychiatrist this man had seen, I couldn't resist observing that the patient also loved to eat therapists. One by one he weighted them down with his Froginess and chuckled over their inability to rise to the surface. To a Frog, that's power!

This Frog takes the Jerk form of Adapted Child. He accepts church positions he can't possibly handle. He lets himself be persuaded to sing a solo although he sings off key. He keeps the church's checkbook and scrambles the figures. "The Church deserves better than me," he likes to say, but just let somebody try to spare him the effort!

There is a third choice for the Frog. He can decide "I'm Not OK and neither is anything or anybody else!" This is the Sulker's basic life position. His life motto, "Don't *go* anywhere, just stew around!" Sammy Sulk leads a life of absolute futility. Every situation is a lose/lose operation. He goes to the polls to vote for the lesser of two undesirables. His decisions are always between "negatives." He likes to say, "Given the situation, what else could I do?" In his world no one ever wins.

Basic life positions (BLPs) are *positions,* not feelings. A BLP is a fundamental conviction about how one will *act* most of the time, regardless of how he feels. We move into and out of each of these positions from time to time, but one will be our predominant way of perceiving ourselves and others.*

Change, solutions, and health will not come unless we are in the OK-OK position. My wife will never hear my side of a problem if I'm seeing her as a Not-OK dumb broad. I won't deal with this problem well if I'm seeing myself as a Not-OK dumb husband. If I think neither of us is worth a hoot, why bother?

Churches forfeit their chances for sharing the gospel when they preach or operate from a Frog's BLP.

---

*Some of us hold that there are only *two* genuine positions: OK-OK and Not OK-Not OK. The other two positions (Not OK-OK and OK-Not OK) are additional ways of operating out of the Not OK-Not OK stance. My conviction: *All* Frogs feel deep down that *no* one is OK, and that's the problem.

OK-NOT OK: I have all the answers and you know nothing. I'm your only hope for salvation.

NOT OK-OK: I don't know why I bother preaching. I'm not sure of myself, and you're living a better life than I am in the first place. But I'll try to meet your expectations.

NOT OK-NOT OK: We're all sinners in a cruddy world. Might as well run this sermon by my sinners one more time. I don't know what else to do.

Some Frongs have more status than others. Regardless of the BLP they have chosen, some are not out-and-out Losers— they're Nonwinners. They are scripted to do so-so, and their lives are "not bad." They're just not allowed to win—ever!

The redeeming thought of a Nonwinner is "at least . . .": "At least I wasn't poor"; "At least I got my kids through college"; "At least our marriage never broke up"; "At least I made it to middle management"; "At least I had a little fun." Beyond that "at least" is a greater goal the individual wanted to reach but didn't.

Both Nonwinners and Losers have *banal scripts*. These people live the sort of lives society approves, but it's a bland existence. I have a fantasy that helps me here. The Winner lies on his deathbed with a grin on his face. "Wow!" he says. "That was really something!" The Loser lies there wondering, "What was *that* all about? Is that all there is?"

By the time a child is from five to seven years old, he has adopted a basic life position, he has made some early traumatic decisions, and he has a head full of "no-no's." Now the problem is how to put it all together into a life program. That's quite a job for a six-year-old.

One day, so TA theory says, the child hears a fairy story, or a nursery rhyme, or a TV program (something with a "story line"), and it all falls into place. "That's who I am and how my life will be!" The newly discovered story line becomes the libretto. It tells the child—and, later, the adult—how life will go.

Losers pick a story like Cinderella. They spend their lives surrounded by "mean, ugly sisters and mothers." Their life task is to do the dirty work and put up with a lot of lip from those around them—and *wait*. They wait for the arrival of a fairy godmother, who is supposed to make all things right. But there is no fairy godmother! At age eighty-five her backsides covered with ashes and her face wrinkled from eight decades of abuse by others—the Loser mumbles to herself, "If that mother with the wings doesn't get here pretty soon, it's going to be too damn late!"

Nonwinners (being a step above Losers) choose a more "productive" script, like "Waiting for Santa Claus." This script, too, requires a lot of effort. The Frog has to find a tree, erect it, and cover it with lights, tinsel, and ornaments. The house, too, must be decorated. When everything is ready, the expectant Frog hides behind the sofa and waits. From time to time he emerges to dust the ornaments, replace dead lights, and freshen Santa's milk and cookies. But mostly he waits.

If Santa does come, the combined weight of all those reindeer, the iron sleigh, and jelly-belly Santa himself will probably crush the roof *and* the waiting Frog. But usually he doesn't come, so a lifetime has been wasted.* Similar scripts are "Waiting for Graduation," "Waiting for Marriage," "Waiting Until the Kids Are Grown," and "Waiting for Retirement." But the plot always turns on waiting for the day "when things will get better." Some Frogs just wait for heaven.

In contrast, Winners pick a script like "Robin Hood." They pick their battles and win them. They know whom they're fighting and why. In between battles they frolic in Sherwood Forest with the maidens. They're never lonely, because the people in the woods form a team; they nurture and nourish each other.

*The details of the "Waiting for Santa Claus" script are Phil Gruenke's.

If you *must* have a script, a Winner's script is preferred; however, abundant life means being script-free. Robin Hood was always fighting the sheriff, whereas a script-free Robin would enjoy having lunch with the sheriff from time to time.

When scripts come to light, I am constantly amazed at their variety. A man seeking therapy for his "inability" to get along with people—he manipulates family members, coworkers, and friends until they finally explode and leave him— reports that his favorite childhood story was "Pinocchio." But he identifies with Geppetto, the puppet *maker*! He loves to manipulate people.

A seminary student is asked who he'd like to be. "I couldn't pick just one, but five: Jesus, Martin Luther King, Bobby Kennedy, Jack Kennedy, and Mahatma Gandhi." This lad won't feel fulfilled until he finds a cross to climb onto.

Script analysis on a twenty-year-old woman revealed these injunctions:

> Don't defend yourself.
> Don't feel important.
> Don't expect much.
> Don't be close to people.
> Don't grow up.
> Don't goof up.
> Don't be sexy.
> Don't trust men.
> Don't show your feelings.
> Don't make waves.
> Don't get married.
> Don't give up.

How's that for a set of marching orders? And her favorite story as a small child was "Sleeping Beauty." Fantastic! The Sleeping Beauty life-image enabled her to comply with every "Don't" in the list, including "Don't give up." For a hundred years Sleeping Beauty hung in there waiting for a prince to come along.

Two characteristics help me to spot "scripty behavior" in myself or others: Scripty living is *relentless* or *repetitive*. Some lives move relentlessly from point A to point B to point C. For instance, a man with a tragic script and an injunction against living had tried to die by getting himself shot in the chest during an armed robbery. "Unfortunately," as he put it, he lived. Now he's spending his sentence planning to do better next time. He knows his wife will play around with other men while he is in prison, and he will kill her for that. He will then kill himself, cheating the state out of an electrocution. He is very clear about this scenario and stubbornly fights options. Relentless!

Other scripts are repetitive. A woman finds a loser, marries him, experiences hell, and gets a divorce. Then she repeats.

A man was telling me he wanted to get rid of the stress in his life. As I listened, I became aware that he himself was creating the stress. His Nurturing Parent would set up a goal for him, but when he acted on this order, his Critical Parent would clobber him for "not doing it well enough."

He had no way to win. Watching for the "clobber," I saw him repeat the exercise four times in ten minutes. His script called for him to place himself between a rock and a hard place and then to explain how he got there. His Child was continuously being "cornered" by his Parent, and every dialogue with another person was an effort to keep himself from being cornered. Invariably he failed. Repetitive!

While acting out a script, we play Games and collect bad feelings. We aren't experiencing and enjoying life *as it happens*; we're someplace else, playing a role. The script, Games, and Rackets prevent us from finding *ourselves* and *life*. But the Child insists that this is the way to keep mom and dad loving him.

In Christian theology this concept (that we build our own hell) has been called "sin." Today the word "sin" is heavily barnacled over with Parent-Child overtones. Sin means we did a no-no. Shame, shame! In earlier days, when God was seen as a big, white-haired granddaddy in the sky, people reacted appropriately to the idea of sin being a no-no. Daddy God became angry and wouldn't give them goodies. Today people are rather indifferent to the notion of a heavenly but picky-picky dispenser of favors, who, incidentally, shows favoritism.

Sin is more than a no-no. It is pain. I like the cartoon of a cow standing on her own udder. The caption reads, "So you think *you've* got troubles!" Sin is like that. We keep ourselves in pain. We keep ourselves away from life. We keep ourselves from moving.

Sin is the bad information about life that we collected back in childhood; it is all the bad decisions and bad feelings we hang onto today. We've called it "original sin" because it comes with being human.* The question is not, How do we avoid this early mess-up? but, How do we escape after it happens? Now that we're civilized and socialized—now that we understand the real world and our place in it—what things must we do in order not to stand on our own udders? What are we doing to keep us from being ourselves? What changes will get a new show on the road—one that provides abundant life?

Losers spend time explaining how they got to be losers, but Winners move on. People don't get well by focusing on how good they are at sinning. A rabbi once shared with me, "You Christians *love* to talk about your sins." Similarly, people in therapy frequently want to talk about how they messed up.

A woman went to a police station to report she had been raped. She gave seven pages of explicit details. When the officer asked the time and date, she acknowledged that the attack happened twenty years earlier.

"Why are you reporting it now?"

"I like to talk about it."

We can either *talk about* our messed-up condition and how we got that way, or we can *change*.

---

*Re "original sin." I see no way to avoid those early crazy decisions that keep us in trouble. Someone, I don't remember who, said that no mother, however perfect, could *ever* give a child the love it needed. The sin *is* original!

Frog scripts produce unnecessary pain. Losers are uncomfortable at best, miserable at worst. When the pain becomes intolerable, these people express a desire to reduce the pain, but there's a hitch: Most losers don't *want* to change. When someone comes to see me about a problematic life, I know he's going to resist change. As miserable as his life may have been, his ways of coping have gotten him this far. It's hard to give up something that works, even if it works poorly.

Sam is tired of his lousy marriage, but he doesn't want to quit yelling at Sally for her silly mistakes—he wants her to quit making them! At work he doesn't want to quit being a quiet, unassuming guy who does all the work—he wants to stay docile *and* find joy in life. Eric Berne's example is a guy who's back in the kitchen standing tiptoe on a stool. His head is in a noose suspended from the light fixture. What he wants is for someone to put a phone book under his feet so he can hang *comfortably*. When he finds a way to *feel* better while continuing to be sick, he announces to his friends, "I'm making progress."

"Progress" is important business to some, but it's the archenemy of health. "Progress" is the Sunday-school superintendent announcing, "This week the seventh graders only tore up *one* classroom." It's getting drunk only twice a week. It's chewing your nails without biting the "quick." "Progress" is a husband and wife learning to hate each other amiably.

Exchanging one nonuseful behavior for another doesn't obliterate the sin—we're still estranged from life. To be healthy, the hanging person must take the noose from around his neck, get off that stool, leave the kitchen, and join the folk in the living room. That is constructive change, not "progress."

The Rich Young Ruler (see Luke 18) wanted to continue "making progress." He asked Jesus what he needed to do to be saved. He had been on a carefully sculpted life program for a long time. He had money and power; he was respected. He saw his life as a pyramid with only the peak missing. "What one thing more must I do . . . ?"

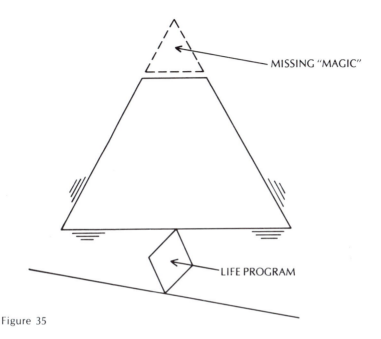

MISSING "MAGIC"

LIFE PROGRAM

Figure 35

His life was shaky, not because the capstone was missing, but because the whole thing rested on a faulty foundation. Jesus knew that the man could add a million "missing pieces" and never get it all together.

I see lots of folk who, like the Rich Young Ruler, seek to find life *without changing.* They try this "magic" and that (yoga, transcendental meditation, the church, astrology, health foods, and now TA), but their basic life program remains the same. Their life is still yukkh!

Christians talk and sing about being "dead to sin." Dying to sin means freeing myself from the crazy idea that the way I've been living is the *only* way I can live. It means siphoning the energy out of my Games and Rackets to use for good stuff.

Jesus invited the Rich Young Ruler to "Sell what you have, give it to the poor folk who can use it, and come follow me."

117

I've heard sermons saying Jesus meant that you can't be happy as long as you have money in the bank; to be a real Christian, you gotta go broke. These pulpiteers missed the point. Jesus was asking the RYR to take a sledge hammer and bust up his entire life and then rebuild it. Abandon all his misconceptions about what matters; give up his standard operating procedures. Find a whole new set of values; reorient his goals. Either this or he wouldn't find salvation. (Sometimes "salvation" is called "being born again." See why? For the RYR, money and social position formed the base of the pyramid. Maybe you've built your life on something else.) The RYR didn't want *change*; he wanted "progress." So he left—"sad," it's recorded.

What TA calls "health," the gospel calls "redemption." Businessmen call it "going back to Square One." For anyone it's trading a worn-out, bent-out-of-shape attempt at life for the real thing. The church says this health follows conversion, or repentance. It comes when you decide to quit following directions that lead nowhere and pursue a different path that leads *somewhere.*

If I intended to fly from Houston to Dallas, but flew on a course of 175 degrees (almost due south), I would soon find myself over the Gulf of Mexico. Knowing there's not that much water on the way to Dallas, I could do either of two things. Following the Protestant Work Ethic—"Work harder!"—I could stay on the same course but fly faster. I would determinedly get to Dallas—by flying 25,000 miles, or all the way around the world! Actually, I would run out of gas. The other option, which makes more sense, is to find a new direction. In TA terms, I would "put a new show on the road." Biblically, I would "convert" my direction.

Biblical folk knew about the possibility of changing scripts. "Though your sins are as scarlet, they will become white as snow" (translated: "Even though you've had forty years' practice at screwing up, you can reverse the trend anytime you decide to"). You don't have to stand on your own udder unless you want to!

Trading your old life in on a new one (redemption), or, failing that, eliminating the effects of the old one (salvation), is ultimately a matter of decision. It's not easy, but it's simple!

All of us are where we are today because of decisions we can do something about. If I'm a loudmouth, then somewhere along the line I decided to use my mouth loudly, and I kept at it because it seemed to help me to survive. If I'm lonely (in a world of 2 billion people) it's because I *decided* to be lonely and know how to make it happen. I could have learned how to avoid loneliness, but why would someone who is "supposed to be lonely" want to learn that?

The concept of change is hard for people to grasp and appreciate because we've been told, "Life's like that, so you might as well accept it." We've been scolded for things we didn't really understand, and we've felt Not OK for so long that it "has to be" the fault of someone "out there." Yet freedom to change is the only concept that offers hope. If my life is based on decisions that I made at age three, and using bad information, at that, then I can *change* those decisions and make new ones. Redemption (health) is having the "scales fall" from our eyes so that we can see reality clearly. "I won't do those crazy things anymore! I'll pick my foot up and quit hurting!"

But—be aware that your Child ego state won't permit this new decision until he's assured everything's going to be all right for him. Your Child has decided to operate in a certain way because that's how he got his fuzzies (or pricklies) in the first place. He's learned to follow whatever script he thinks will bring him strokes. So, before you can make a helpful new decision, you have to determine what your Child is getting out of the old behavior and give him something else.

Getting rid of scripts that lead nowhere begins with a determination to live in the here-and-now. This inevitably leads us to examining our ingrained bad feelings. Let's push on and see what our emotions are really like.

10

The Rackets: I Can Feel
Worse Than You Can

Our feelings often make or break us. This chapter can change your life. The contents changed mine! At the heart of it is the Martian observation that you are responsible for (able to control) everything inside your own skin.

Early in life the Child inside you was convinced that people can manipulate one another's feelings. "He *made* me mad!" "You *make* me feel guilty." As children we believed the other person somehow had the magical power to produce an emotion within us. The fact is, no person can control another's emotions. Sam insults Sally, but he does not *make* her feel bad. His put-down is only an *invitation* for her to feel bad. She can, if she chooses, turn down his invitation and feel whatever she wants.

We think what we think because *we think it*. I acknowledge I'm responsible for the invitation that I give other people, but I cannot be response-able for what others decide to feel. *They* choose.

Have you ever tried to make someone angry and had him laugh at you, or have you tried to cheer someone up only to have her grow sadder and sadder? We spend too much time futilely trying to control the emotions and actions of others, while we spend too little time getting in touch with our own emotions, which we *can* control.

In TA, feelings are divided into three groups (the Three R's): reactions, rubber bands, and Rackets.

A reaction is an authentic emotional response of the Natural Child to a here-and-now stimulus:

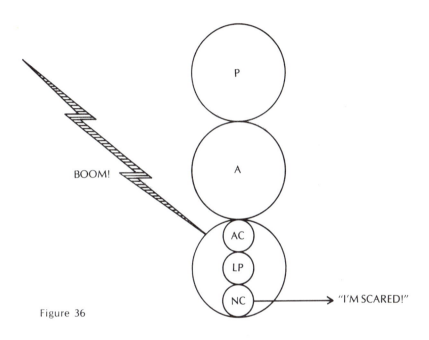

Figure 36

Lightning crashes and he feels scared. He sees a dog run over by a car and he feels sad. He sees a rainbow and he feels joy. He gets his foot caught under a chair and feels frustrated. A car brushes him and he experiences anger.

In each instance the feeling is immediate and is in direct response to something that *happens*. Genuine reactions are short-lived; they cannot be sustained without repeated stimuli. At a funeral friends experience grief for several minutes, then find themselves laughing together. Later, upon viewing the casket, they experience grief again. I bang my shin and feel angry with myself until the pain stops, whereupon I'm at peace with myself again.

We call a second kind of emotion a rubber band. It's stretched between the past and present. Today I experience an event that closely resembles a traumatic experience in the past. My emotions spring back, as a stretched rubber band might, to that earlier scene.

For example, I'm walking along at dusk on a crisp November evening. From an open window floats the smell of pot roast. *Z-i-n-g*! I'm no longer in Texas, but in Indiana delivering the evening paper. I'm about to go home to Mamma Edna's table. I can feel the way the house felt, smell the smell, see it all. Obviously I am not *that* deeply affected by any here-and-now stimulus. I have rubber-banded! My response is out of proportion to the immediate smell. I am re-experiencing feelings of twenty-five years ago.

We rubber-band in a negative way, too. The boss calls on the phone: "Would you step over to my office for a moment?" Ninety-nine times out of a hundred he merely wants some information or wants to hand me an assignment. For me, however, there's a rubber band—if only for a second. "Oh, oh. I'm in trouble!" During that moment, I have been summoned not by my boss, but by my principal, and I re-experience the terror of a seven -year-old on his way to get "justiced" by the God of the Whole Entire School.

Since we get into rubber-band situations from time to time, it's helpful to know about them. While rubber-banding, we can't really solve anything. We're "back there." An acquaintance sees me but fails to nod or otherwise say hello. *Bang*! I feel put-down. A genuine reaction might be irritation or disappointment, or even amusement, but I'm rubber-banding, overreacting. His stimulus rocketed me back to days when I'd go out to play and the other kids wouldn't have anything to do with me. Those kids aren't around anymore, but my friend is. I need to come out of the rubber band and investigate why he didn't nod. I may discover he was preoccupied—or, it could be he's angry with me and we need to talk. Coming to either conclusion permits me to act in the here-and-now. Staying in the rubber band can wipe out the whole day, a whole week, or a whole friendship.

Sometimes we have genuine reactions, sometimes we rubber-band, and sometimes we experience what we call a Racket. (Eric Berne gave us the concept of "Rackets and Trading Stamps." The notion of rubber bands came from David Kupfer and Morris Haimowitz.*)

There are many unpleasant ways your Child can feel, including mad, sad, anxious, insecure, worried, depressed, lonely, frustrated, hurt, guilty, afraid, disappointed, irritated, or incompetent. Each *can be* an immediate response to a here-and-now stimulus, or a rubber band; however, most of the bad feelings we experience in ourselves and in others are neither spontaneous nor involuntary—they are *learned.* They are also manipulative. Rackets are a way we have found to play Emotional One-Upmanship with those around us. TA practitioners believe that most bad feelings are unnecessary, that we can reduce the amount of time we feel bad by 90 percent—unless we *like* feeling bad. My TA Parent tape tells me feeling good is better than feeling bad. (No one can prove that; it's a bias.) Unfortunately, most of us have learned that bad feelings are a very powerful tool. A Martian would notice immediately that we continually set ourselves up to feel bad.

A Racket is a chronic conspiracy between your Parent and your Child to feel bad in a particular way and for your own purposes. Here's how I think it happened:

---

*Dave Kupfer, now dead, was Berne's close friend. Morris Haimowitz and his wife, Natalie, are TA trainers and theoreticians in the Chicago area.

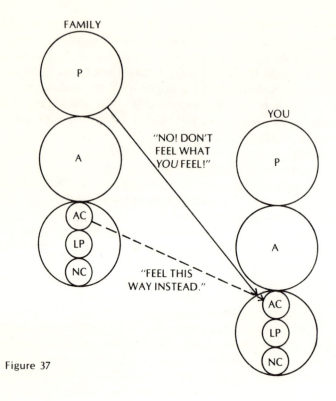

Figure 37

When you were a little tyke, you had a full range of emotions going in your Natural Child; however, your family (like most families) did not *allow* many of these feelings. Families have a way of deciding, without much real thought, to authorize only a few bad feelings around the homestead.

For example, you were three years old and your mother put you to bed. You had teddy bear, but he wasn't saying much. You couldn't get off to sleep. You heard laughter and music from the living room, and suddenly you became aware of your apartness. In that dark bedroom all by yourself, you felt lonely. (Makes sense so far.) You grabbed teddy bear, stuck your thumb in your mouth, and went into the living room. "I'm lonesome!" you reported. Whoops! Mistake! Lonely wasn't an authorized feeling in your family.

"How can you be lonely? The house is full of people. You have your teddy bear to talk to, and you love teddy. You can't be lonely."

Again you tried to express what you were feeling, but it became evident that you weren't *supposed* to do a lonely in that house. You knew there was *something* going on in your gut. You thought you were "lonely," but were you wrong? You began observing the other kids. Sure enough, none ever acted lonely. (Or for you maybe it was being scared that wasn't authorized. "How can you be scared in such a safe house, blah, blah?")

What *was* it okay for me to feel? When I looked around my home, I discovered that all the other Kids were doing hurts. Having your feelings hurt was authorized, and everyone was doing it except mom, who did anxiouses instead. That was a break: Whenever I felt lonely or scared, I could do a hurt as a substitute. To be sure, everyone's *Parent* disapproved ("You shouldn't feel hurt; no one wants to hurt you"), but just the same, their *Child* was always *doing* a hurt. It was like seeing a "No Smoking" sign in a classroom but observing that even the professor was smoking. We do what the other Kids do.

This newly learned, family-authorized feeling, then, became a substitute for genuine reactions. I found that my new Racket was useful; it had some power. Instead of being lonely, I could crank up a hurt and march into the living room flashing it as my passport. With my lip hanging down to the floor and manufactured tears flowing from my eyes, I would say in a quivering voice, "Why do you people love each other more than you love me? It hurts my feelings to be forced to be all alone while you're having so much fun." (I don't remember how three-year-olds say that, but they manage.) This time, because I employed the family-sanctioned Racket, Mom and

Dad and the rest immediately did a guilty. They even popped the cap off a root beer and shoved it into my hand to compensate for their bad behavior. The Racket worked.

Note that the cranked-up, phony hurt *feels* like the real thing. The brain and body operate the same way in all three forms of emotion. Note also that the lonesome youngster with the teddy bear could have used another Racket, like worrying about the house burning down. Or, a collector of angries could do a hostile to cover his loneliness.

These rackety bad feelings, learned from the family, are collected and used with regularity in subsequent situations. *Any* situation. With bad feelings we can "buy" things that we don't have Parental permission to have except at the expense of feeling guilty. TA refers to this buying operation as collecting "Trading Stamps."

With bad-feelings Trading Stamps you can purchase three classes of things: toys, minor prizes, and major prizes.

A toy is something you could "afford" to buy if only you had permission. A toy is getting stoned drunk or buying a suit of clothes you "really don't need." A toy is skipping work to go fishing or letting the housework go until tomorrow. Since you're a "grown-up," you could *afford* any of the above—that is, have them without suffering harm.

You want a new fishing rod and you've already decided to get one. You've got the money but not the permission. Either your wife or your Parent says, "Oh, no you don't! Sam Junior needs braces on his teeth; besides, you're behind on your church pledge." No permission! So you start collecting bad-feelings Stamps, and when you have a full book, you'll trade it in on your fishing rod and not feel guilty.

Let's say you're a collector of angry Stamps. How to get the fishing rod? Sit down to eggs and remember that a week ago you told your wife you were hungry for French toast. She hasn't delivered. Mad, mad, mad! Three Stamps, right there! You go out and notice your son's bike lying on the lawn. It's been there before, but now you can *use* its neglect. Mad, mad, mad! See how it goes? By five o'clock you have collected three and a half books of mads. "With a day like I've had, I deserve to do something for myself!" Off to the discount store for the fishing rod.

People who collect real trading stamps (the kind the stores pass out) know where to shop. They know every store in town that "gives away" (boy, is that a myth!) their favorite brand of stamps.

Let me show you how proficient people are at collecting phony emotions. I was a collector of hurts. By the time I was twenty I was really good at collecting them. On a bad day (when hurts were scarce), I could get hurt over the tone a person used to say "Good morning." By age forty I could do exquisite hurts from scratch. God how "they hurt me!" When everything else fails, a good Racketeer can counterfeit a bad-feelings Stamp. Ever say something innocuous to another person and have him get mad? He needed four more Stamps to fill a book, and, getting none, he ran off some counterfeits.

When I became aware of how hard I was working in order to hurt (and how much time I was spending—time that I could use for fun things), I quit. It took a lot of attention but wasn't really difficult—it wasn't as hard as collecting and carrying around that burden of bad feelings. It was also fun to get in touch with the real emotions (reactions) that lay dormant under my Rackety hurts.

I hadn't done a hurt in months when the following drama took place. A statewide church meeting was coming up, and Barbara and I intended to go. Ordinarily I looked forward to seeing our friends. And the trip itself was fun. However, this year the meeting place was Seguin, Texas, which isn't exactly San Francisco. Also, a fight was brewing on some stupid issue, and I didn't feel like fighting. Besides, I would have to cancel some speaking engagements. One night, before falling asleep, I decided I wouldn't go.

Next morning, as I stumbled to the kitchen for my life-restoring cup of coffee, I recalled my decision. And what did I find in the kitchen? No hot water. Barbara hadn't put on the hot water! Boy, did that hurt! I'm a good husband. I do a lot of things for Barbara. I don't ask much from her. But I do expect her to heat water for my coffee. That isn't asking too much, now is it? You'd think that if she really loved me . . . Hurt, hurt!

Defeated in the kitchen, I stumbled off to the bathroom. On the way, I stopped at the door of Julie's bedroom and called, "Good morning, darling," No answer! I love that little girl. I do a lot for her. And I don't ask much of her either. But I do expect her to say "Good morning." Hurt, hurt!

By then the little red flag in the back of my head popped up. "Arthur, you don't collect hurts anymore, remember? But you've just got yourself two sets of Stamps in two minutes flat. What's going on?"

I went into the bathroom and flushed down the hurt Stamps. It only took two seconds for the chemical reaction I had stirred up to go away. While I was shaving, I got in touch with my innards. What had I really been feeling that I'd replaced with those phony hurts?

I had been feeling lonely! That made sense. By not going to the conference, I would miss all the fun-and-games. I'd miss the after-hours parties where we swap lies and jokes, and play our guitars and sing far into the night. I'd miss all the gossip, usually referred to as "News of the Lord's Work in Other Fields." And my buddies might not even miss me! I felt lonely!

Now that I was in touch with the real reaction, loneliness, I decided to allow myself to experience this until I finished shaving; then I would go find some family members to love. Once I got into my lonely, it dissipated in about two minutes. Real feelings don't last very long. The rest of the morning went great. But what if I'd stayed with my Racket? Chaos!

Remember, loneliness is an emotion I don't have much practice experiencing; we just never did a lonely back in Indiana. Also, I was vulnerable because I was fresh out of bed and my Parent and Adult had not yet awakened, so TA wasn't there to help. But my Child was awake—it's the last one to go to sleep at night and the first one awake in the morning. Early and late are good times to get to know your Child. My Child did what he had always done to cover an authentic lonely feeling: He did a hurt.

In retrospect I saw that those Stamps I'd collected were phonies. Actually, Barb almost never puts the water on—she's too busy making sandwiches, collecting stuff for the kids, handing out milk money. Besides, she isn't wild about coffee, so she doesn't remember it in the rush. I'm the one who usually puts the coffee water on. (When I relieve Barb and do all those chores, I myself forget the coffee.) The only time there's a hot-water issue is when I need to do a feel-bad. And as for Julie, she never talks to anyone until she's up and dressed and has washed her face. My Kid had gone where he knew he would *not* get something, whereupon he could do a hurt instead of a lonely.

One of the places your Child can go to collect bad-feelings Stamps is groups designed for "sharing real feelings." The group members are supposed to "encounter" one another. Often such a group, if presided over by untrained "leaders," keeps working until everyone has collected the Stamps he wants.

When Mr. Fluster came to our TA group, he reported he had been going to an encounter group for five years. I wouldn't go to the same dermatologist for five years even if I had eczema, seborrhea, and psoriasis all at once! His wife had already told me that he came home from these sessions as angry as a hornet and would stay angry for two or three days. I figured it must have been important for him to get mad, and my hunch was correct. After four weeks in our group without collecting any mads, he left. ("I'm sorry, but the group isn't quite what I had in mind. It isn't doing for me what I thought it' would.") Eric Berne said sensitivity groups are where sensitive people go to have their feelings hurt. I think he was right. Later I found that Mr. F. belonged simultaneously to three other groups—all of which "made him angry"—and *paid* for the privilege!

Many people feel they aren't being "honest" except when

they let their *bad* feelings show. "Groupies"—people who love to join groups so they can feel good by feeling bad—discount *good* feelings. Actually, a group that laughs and giggles and feels joyous is just as honest as folk who share their fears. But I digress.

Not everyone collects bad-feelings Trading Stamps to spend on *toys.* Some ignore toys and save up for a minor prize. A minor prize is one you *can't* afford, either with or without permission. A minor prize is not two martinis for a Baptist or getting drunk one night for an Episcopalian—it's a two-week bender! It's running off with someone for ten days of sex and not telling your family where you are. It's going on a shopping rampage with the credit cards and getting yourself hopelessly in debt. It's a suicide *attempt.* (You're not allowed to kill yourself as a minor prize—you don't have that many Stamps yet.)

Some people (estimated roughly at 5 percent of the population by some guy who likes to estimate roughly) pass over minor prizes and save their stamps until they can have a major prize. There are only four:

> *Suicide:* the ultimate get-away-from position.
> *Homicide:* the ultimate get-rid-of position.
> *Other "Major Quits":* like divorce or "leaving the ministry." Here it isn't the action, but the *context.* A Frog quits to get even; a Winner would get a divorce or change occupations without collecting feel-bads first.
> *Institutionalization:* convincing society you must be imprisoned; convincing a physician you can play crazy well enough to be put away; or having your stomach removed to eliminate the bleeding ulcer. This is the ultimate get-nowhere position.

However useful real trading stamps may be to merchants and our economy, somebody has to pay for the paper, the printing, the perforating, the glue, the covers and their printing, the staples, the little dispensing machines, and the redemption centers and their activities, not to mention the merchandise. I don't think all this is being paid for by the stamp company. For years stores have been saying these stamps are free, but during a recent dollar crisis some stores announced they were eliminating them to lower their prices. Aha! And when you turn in your stamps, you still have to pay the tax—in cash; they won't accept stamps for tax. On the way home, you pass discount stores selling the same item. You remember the countless hours you spent collecting and licking those damn stamps and how hard it was to get the glue out of your mouth. And you ask yourself, "The fishing rod was *free*?"

Emotional Trading Stamps work the same way. Do an experiment right now. Put down the book and frown. Pretend you're really angry with someone. Pay attention to your face muscles, how they feel. Now smile. Pay attention to your face. Notice the difference? Smiling is much easier.

Remember the last time you did a barn-burning, fist-pounding mad? The kind it took you a week to prepare for? When you finally got over it, how did you feel? Exhausted! It takes a lot of energy to crank up a mad or a hurt. Remember the time your spouse "made you mad" and you decided to give it to her/him, and she/he was *late*? To keep the mad going, you had to keep going back over the material. That's a lot of wasted energy. "I couldn't help myself. He *made* me angry." Wrong! You invested a bunch of your life in staying angry. Working a Racket isn't easy or "natural," no matter what your Parent says.

Phil Gruenke (you remember he introduced me to TA) told me a story illustrating how people marry to perpetuate their Stamp collection. A woman who likes to play "Bitch and Nag" looks around until she finds a man who plays "Drunk and Proud of It." They marry and have a nice, symbiotic relationship. She bitches and nags all week, and by Friday he has enough Stamps to spend the weekend drinking. Stays drunk, stays away. "You'd drink too if you were married to *her*," he says to bar-buddies. All weekend she's collecting Stamps. "Why isn't he home? Why am I treated this way?" When, finally, he comes home early Monday morning, she has a couple of books full of Stamps, enough to finance another week of "Bitch and Nag." "You'd complain too if you were married to *him*," she tells her friends.

Then their mutual arrangement hit a snag. He decided to sober up. Stayed sober for six months. He became a "model husband." She went on collecting Stamps from all her other sources, but *she couldn't use them on him anymore*! Guess what happened? Right! She divorced him. Earth-people have trouble figuring this one. Why would she divorce him now that he's a model husband? Martians understand. Not being able to spend her stamps on "Bitch and Nag," she suddenly found herself with 150 books in the closet-in-her-head. She didn't want to kill him or kill herself, and she didn't want to be locked up, so the only other prize was a "major quit," and she took it.

Six months later she remarried. Who this time? Right again! Another drunk. She had learned from her mistake, though. This time she married a full-time drunk. When asked how her new marriage is working, she complains, "It's terrible! He beats me!" Life is back to "normal." "God takes care of idiots and fools," someone said. I think we take care of ourselves pretty well.

Hard-core Stamp collectors really hang in there. I watched a woman who wanted to work on her "problem" of worrying so much.

"What do you do when you aren't worrying?"

"I worry about why I'm not worrying!"

Another question.

Silence.

"What are you thinking about now?"

"I'm worried. I can't think of the right answer!"

She was good at it!

Perhaps you're wondering if *you* have a Racket going. If so, what is it? There are two ways of spotting a Racket. The first is to answer the question, "Of all the bad feelings I experience, which is the most prominent—the one I spend the most time feeling?"

Statistically it doesn't make sense that of all the emotions experienced by a human being I should spend so much time feeling hurt. With fifteen or twenty possible bad feelings, I was spending two-thirds of my bad-feelings time hurt. A Racket!

Since a genuine emotion doesn't last long and is directly tied to a here-and-now stimulus, a Racket can be suspected when you still feel bad hours or days after the immediate stimulus has passed. If I come home "angry as hell" about an incident that happened this morning at work, it's because I have remembered the stimulus over and over again.

"I can't forget it!" you say? The heck you can't. If you're like me, you're all too good at forgetting things that matter. If it wasn't *important* to you, you wouldn't remember this offending event. You're saving it—for something in exchange.

To live, you have to eat; and to eat, you have to put up with the garbage. It comes with the living. As we live, there are bound to be frustrations, disappointments, anxious times, things to worry about, frights, loneliness. There's no way to live without experiencing some bad feelings, some garbage. The only way you can totally avoid garbage is to live on vitamin pills. (That's living?) "We haven't had a cross word in forty years." They probably haven't spoken to each other—at least they haven't *said* anything! No communication, no garbage. Ugh!

The Winner eats his dinner, then scrapes the corn cob and chicken bones into the garbage pail, where they belong. "Now, what's next in life to do? I'm not going to spend any time thinking about that garbage!"

The Winner has three ways for getting rid of garbage (bad feelings). The best way is to give it back to the person who contributed to it. Jesus said that if you go to church to worship, get in touch with the deeper parts of your life. If you remember you have something against your brother, put your offering envelope down and go back home and get this thing settled between you and your brother, then come back and put your envelope in the offering plate (Matthew 5:23-24). Jesus said you can't find God (or anything else that's worthwhile) if you're saving your garbage. The Winner goes to the other guy and says, "Hey, I really felt disappointed when you told me (etc., etc.). I want you to know what I felt, and that now I'm feeling good about it." Flush, flush. The garbage is gone.

If you can't or won't tell the "offender," you can go the second route—tell it to your priest or whoever does "priesting" for you. It might be anyone. Tell them about the incident. I'm convinced "confession of sin" is a beautiful way to ditch garbage. "There! I've got it out. Now I'm ready to move on."

Third, if you just refuse to talk about it to anybody, you can do your own flushing in your very own head. Resolve, "It's gone!" and act like it.

Caution: You can't dump garbage in any of these ways as long as a conspiracy exists between your Parent and Child to feel bad.

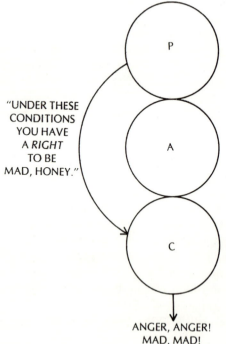

"UNDER THESE CONDITIONS YOU HAVE A *RIGHT* TO BE MAD, HONEY."

P

A

C

ANGER, ANGER! MAD, MAD!

Figure 38

The Loser (Frog) has permission to feel bad, so after dinner he collects his own garbage and then goes around and collects everybody else's. He makes sure he has every last piece, even from under the toaster and behind the canisters. He uses a checklist. He carefully carries all the garbage into the living room and dumps it on the coffee table. Back to the kitchen for a Baggie. Now the Frog stuffs all the garbage into the Baggie—and ties the Baggie to his belt!

He likes to keep his Baggie of garbage handy because there's so much to do with it. If his wife bugs him, he can show her how many bags of crud he's got strapped to him. While drinking coffee, he and the boys can play show-and-tell with their garbage collections: "Let me tell you what *my* wife did to *me.* . . ." "You think *that's* bad? How about what my boss did to me. . . ." Stink, stink, stink. I know someone who filled a garbage bag back in 1933, and he still trots it out now and then. Forty-year-old garbage is ripe!

When you take real trading stamps to the redemption center, you surrender them and you take the prize home with you. But emotional Stamps aren't handed in—they're merely canceled. You get to take them home and put them into the "used Stamp" compartment of the drawer where you keep pieces of string and bent nails. You can always open the drawer (or garbage bag) and show people "how much I've suffered."

In 1972 I was teaching this concept to some great senior-high adults at a Disciples' summer camp. At the closing worship celebration, they translated the idea into a skit. One kid was carrying around an enormous trash bag. Finally, he decided it wasn't worth the effort, so he ditched it. But as he walked away, a long cord payed out from his belt, and soon the bag was trailing him—twenty feet behind, but *there if he needed it.* Another kid threw away a garbage bag marked *See how my roommate slighted me.* But he began missing his garbage, so, with an empty bag in hand, he went looking for his roommate to get another load.

We save aches and pains for emergency use. The gospel says

(and transactional analysis believes) that this is a dumb way to live. We could use our precious energy in more pleasing, more profitable, more helpful ways.

I'd like to show you a way I've found to short-circuit the garbage-collecting, garbage-toting operation. One evening I arrived home feeling crabby. This was getting to be a habit. I spent some time asking myself what decision I had been making to guarantee my getting home feeling crabby. Answer: I had decided I was going to get home in a hurry or I'd be crabby. Not much of an option, actually. My office is fifteen miles away by freeway, and the "evening rush" lasts from three till eight. No way to get home in a hurry. So I was crabby.

Time to make a new decision. That didn't take much work, either. These three people and a dog that I live with are very favorite friends. Of all the people that I want to "look good" around, they're foremost. New decision: I'm going to get home feeling cheery, no matter what it takes!

Boy, did that ever change things. I have a whole new mission. Some days I leave the office before the traffic builds up and surprise my family with an extra hour I can devote to them. I seek enjoyment while on the road. I see how clever a driver I can be. Sometimes I "write" a sermon or figure out a problem. Sometimes I take letters off license plates and try to make words out of them. (Try RXB.) Being a Peeping Tom during traffic jams is both fun and legal. One night I saw this gorgeously attired, bejeweled, society-matronish woman picking her nose. I giggled all the way home. Sometimes I argue with advertising signs. They yell at me, so why shouldn't I get *my* time in? If all else fails, I tune in one of our country-and-western stations. The song titles alone keep me happy: "Nothin's too good for my wo-o-o-man, and nothin's whut she gets from me!" "I cain't hold my likker, so I've no right ta hold you."

Decisions can set you up for feeling *bad*—or for feeling *good*.

In the course of becoming socialized and civilized, most of us have been brainwashed into believing we shouldn't feel what we feel. We have learned to substitute "acceptable" feelings for what we're actually feeling. Back there, to gain acceptance from those giants around us, we learned to deny the Natural Child feelings and replace them with Adapted Child "feelings":

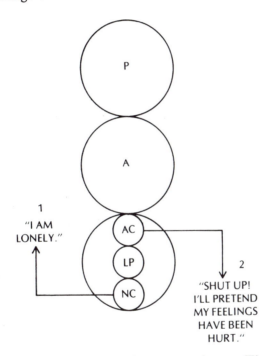

Figure 39

The Adapted Child's Rackets are phony. They are a response to the question "What *must* I 'feel' in order for everyone around here to accept me?"

To learn to live in the now, we must learn to accept our *own* experiences! I have a right to feel what I feel! If I'm feeling lonely, I really don't give two hoots in the Hot Place whether I *should* feel lonely or not; I don't care whether it makes sense; I don't care whether or not most people would feel lonely if they were in my shoes. The fact is, they *aren't* in my shoes; *I'm* in my shoes. And you're in *your* shoes. We feel what we feel. You can't deal with what you should do until you get in touch with what you're doing.

If I could convey only one message to you, it would be this: You have the right to be you. You are the only "you" God ever created. Make the most of it.

11
When One of Us
Has to Lose

A favorite pastime of young people on Okinawa is a circular version of volleyball. One person in the circle bats the ball up, and the idea is to keep it in the air as long as possible. When the ball falls to the ground, the whole group is chagrined.

"What's the fun in that?" I wondered as I watched. "Don't they know someone's supposed to win and someone's supposed to lose?"

It dawned on me that our Western win/lose orientation makes sense only in a sports contest, a war, or keeping a burglar out of the home. But if you're talking about the rest of life, the "somebody's got to lose" mentality makes for tough living. These Oriental folk understood this. They wanted everyone to go home feeling good.

A simulation game taught me the destructiveness of win/lose situations. Each player represented a mythical country, and he was responsible for insuring that his nation had enough to eat. We fiercely gathered our quotas. One by one, nations fell because of starvation. It didn't take long for us to realize that we would all die unless we cooperated from a win/win position. We got together and put an end to starvation.

By age four most people have already been taught to believe someone must lose. "If Sammy gets what he wants, then I must lose—so I'd better stomp Sammy!" With everyone else in the family operating this way, we get lots of help learning to "win."

Quite early in TA, analysts became aware of some consistent transactions that require one or both of the two people to lose, and "Game analysis" was born.

When Eric Berne wrote *Transactional Analysis in Psychotherapy* in 1961 to explain his theory to the Freudian psychoanalytic community, word quickly came back that his theory was clear except for his "Games." Would he clarify? As a secondary resource for therapists he wrote *Games People Play,* and it sold a jillion copies. My hunch is that people were eager to learn some *new* Games to play. New Games emerged—like Game Spotting. The person who was "It" (who had read the book) went to parties and watched for Games; when he saw one, he clobbered the guy doing it and scored two points. His friend went home angry, while "It" went home wondering why he had chosen such dumb friends.

I am not interested in helping people to play more and better Games, nor am I interested in helping someone to expose another's Games. Games are important to us until we find another way to reach our goals. If you strip me of my favorite Games, you leave me vulnerable and desolate. I play them because they help me survive, so I've learned to be good at them. When I play them I always "win." When deprived of *my* Games, I'm forced to play games I *don't* know how to play, and I lose. When people have no way to go, they get desperate. Suicide is a possibility.

A young seminarian told me he was starting a "TA group" with himself as leader. His experience and qualifications? He had read *Games People Play.* He planned to teach people about Games, and then they would sit around and spot one another's. My prediction was that if his group hung together very long, he would have some folk in tough straits.

(TA "book reviewers" and "imitation therapists" are a dime a dozen today. Anyone can gather a crowd. This is great if only *knowledge* is involved. But if the person or group purports to do therapy or to help you to change, you may want to check credentials. Have they been trained by certified people or are they "self-made"?)

Understanding Game theory can be useful in two ways. First, you can spot the Games that *you* initiate. As you become aware of the massive "end run" you're engaged in, you can begin finding straighter ways to achieve the same goal. Your Game will fall by the wayside, unneeded. Second, you can spot a Game when *other people* offer one, but rather than expose it, simply decline to play.

Let me enlarge on this last point. People frequently ask me if refusal is destructive to the other person. The answer is no. Since his Game isn't exposed, he isn't left trapped. He may become frustrated and try harder and harder to get you to play, but sooner or later he'll understand you won't play and he'll look elsewhere. Somebody else will play with him, that's for sure. But with you, he'll either have to come straight or leave you alone. No one is ever hurt when people refuse to engage in "sickness" with them. Since my Games get me in trouble (perpetuate my problems, keep me from the abundant life), you do me a favor when you refuse to play.

So, what's a "Game"?

We aren't talking about bridge, checkers, football. In these the players understand the rules; they know the other side's intentions. In football each team knows the other side wants to beat them, will attempt to trick them, and they know they are supposed to fight back. It's clear. In TA language, football players are engaged in an "activity"—not a "Game."

Games are filled with ulterior transactions. The players appear to be doing one thing, but are intent on doing something entirely different. These sneaky transactions move to a very predictable end, so each player is expected to move in a set progression. They are called "Games" because of this orderliness. Each move is expected to be followed by a particular response.

There are three ways you can spot a Game. First, a Game (or a Game "segment") always ends with both players "feeling bad." The feeling may range from slight irritation—to a door-slamming, dish-breaking, tears-flowing burst of anger. Anytime you and another person both feel bad after a conversation, be aware that something was going on besides what you thought you were doing. You've just played a game.

Second, a game always involves a *discount* of some sort. "How would *you* know? You're just a woman!" This discounts the woman's ability to think. "If I told my husband what I think, it would destroy him" discounts the husband's ability to survive as a human being. "You don't understand the problem" discounts the other person's expressed thought. "I just can't think" discounts my own abilities.

Discounts come in a hundred thousand forms, but once you get the feel for them you see them readily. Jacqui Schiff says discounts fall into four major groupings:*

> 1. We can discount the *problem*: "I'm *not* angry, dammit!"
>
> 2. We can discount the *importance* of the problem: "Sure, I'm mad, but it's not important."
>
> 3. We can discount the *solvability* of the problem: "I know my wife's unhappy, but there's nothing to be done for her."
>
> 4. We can discount *our own ability* to solve the problem: "I don't know how to talk to her about that."

Some other popular discounts:
> "I can't control my emotions."
> "If it weren't for him I'd be happy."
> "I don't know what's right."
> "You don't *really* hate him!"
> "My kids are impossible."
> "Everything's fine!" (Said by a man with a mammoth marital problem.)

---

*Jacqui's article, "Passivity," *Transactional Analysis Journal,* I, no. 1 (January 1971), 71-78, is a "must" for advanced TA scholars. She deals with passivity, symbiosis, and discounts.

Steve Karpman gave us a third way to spot a Game in progress. Since Games are dramas with a plot, they require actors. Steve identified three major roles, two of which must be present for a game to progress: the Rescuer, the Persecutor, and the Victim. Anytime you feel that you want to Rescue someone, or are being victimized, or want to hit someone, a Game is involved. The same for just being invited to play any of these roles.*

Remember that little kid who invaded his parents' cocktail party and beat on the coffee table with a block? He was looking for strokes. Strokes are one of the reasons we play Games. A good Game of "Family Uproar" provides a lot of cold pricklies for everyone involved. This little kid obviously didn't have permission to ask for strokes in a straightforward way, so he plays "Kick Me" instead. After ten or twelve *bang-bang's* on the table, one or both parents want to kick him, and he gets his strokes (literally). The loudmouth in your coffee klatch plays the same Game—and you want to kick him. Boy, do you want to kick him! "Kick Me" players are good at getting themselves kicked.

An expert at playing "Poor Little Me" is good at getting people to Rescue him. Halfway through his story you want to Rescue him from the baddies that are lurking around. Sometimes he produces a baddie right there in the group. He seduces someone into Victimizing him so that other group members will jump to his Rescue. Someone has to lose.

This Rescuer-Victim-Persecutor concept is a handy tool for staying out of offered Games. We avoid Games when we decide never to play any of these three roles:

> "I will not 'Rescue' other people from things they could handle themselves."
> "I will not be Victimized."
> "I will not Persecute."

---

*Karpman introduced his "Drama Triangle" in the *Transactional Analysis Bulletin*, VII, no. 26 (April 1968), 39-43.

The person who is asking for a kick (or asking to be Rescued or Persecuting someone) is really up to something else—something that pays off for himself. Mother is acting out a life script that requires her to be "harried." Her role is "to do everything for everyone else." She carefully arranges to be overloaded. She "suffers" a lot. She could put an end to much of her suffering, but she is *supposed* to be Mother Martyr, the Compleat Victim.

She's been out shopping and the station wagon is full of groceries. Grocery shopping can be fun, but this mom wouldn't let that happen—she's collecting disappointment Stamps. As she pulls into the driveway, she sees her husband headed to the neighbors' house. Her Little Professor recognizes the chance for a Game. "Come help me with the groceries," she calls with fake cheeriness. She *knows* what the answer will be and where the conversation is headed. "Get one of the kids to help you, I'm busy!" comes the answer, as expected. Shafted again! Pout, pout. Anger, disappointment. She got a lot done in one transaction.

Games pay off in Stamps. Look what this good lady accomplished. She was able to "prove" once more that she has to be harried and overworked—there's no possibility for a change. She can use this condition to control family conversations when she needs to. If she needs to hit her husband a lick, she can recall his unwillingness to help her. "You *never* help me!" Her husband, feeling guilty, may bring home a box of candy or let her buy that new rug "to make it up to you." And she can use this example when she and the girls play "See How Husbands Are."

Repeated noneffective actions are highly suspect as Game moves. Like screaming. Sometimes screaming really gets the job done and you always know when it's going to work. You want silence and you yell "Shut up!" from your Most Potent Parent. Everyone in the room turns to stone. Now you can graciously say what you wanted to say. It worked. But most screaming doesn't work. You scream and the kid keeps on writing on the wall. You scream again—same results. After enough screams, you get to do a free whomp on his head. After hitting him, you walk away feeling "incompetent." A Martian would decide screaming is important to you—more important than keeping the wall clean.

Games have a minimum of four parts: A Hook (or Con), a Handle, a Switch, and a Payoff.

The Hook, or Con, is the invitation to play. The Victim's invitation ("I just don't know what to do about my wife") appeals to Rescuing Parents. They hear the unspoken ending to that sentence, ". . . because I'm so helpless, dumb, and unable to handle my life." With this invitation to play, if they *need* to Rescue the other person, they will grab the Handle and help sink the Hook in their own stomach. A Game progresses only when the second person agrees to play. Once both parties are firmly attached to the Game, it progresses until "It," the initiator, decides to throw the Switch. Throwing the Switch means he switches roles—for example, he shifts from Victim to Persecutor, and/or he switches ego states, and/or he switches to his basic life position. Usually he does several of these at once.

An example: Mrs. Fangschleister comes to her pastor, Reverend Bodelschwing, "for help." Mrs. F is an inveterate player of NIGYYSOB, "Now I've Got You, You S.O.B.," which is the major game played by people whose BLP is "I'm OK, you're Not OK" and by Persecutors. Her Little Professor knows that Reverend B. loves to play "I'm Only Trying To Help" and "tries to help" every chance he gets.

"Try" is a Con word. A person saying "I will try" is also saying, "I won't make it, but if I do, boy, will I ever be surprised!" Properly used, "try" means to experiment: "I'll try speaking more loudly to see if people hear me more clearly." I don't hear "try" used legitimately very often. As a Con word, "try" is the Jerk's prediction of failure: "I'll try to come to your party" (meaning "Look for me when and if you see me"). People who like to "try" pay more attention to how hard they are trying than to results.

Reverend Bodelschwing is a "tryer." God didn't call him

into the ministry for results, but to try. We all know how stubborn sinners are, don't we? "God will love me," he tells himself, "if I try." "At least you tried, my son," the Parent in his head says. That same Parent also says, "Try, try again." Being covered with sweat is important.

Reverend B. also works from the "I'm OK, you're Not OK" position. He's the one who has been to college for seven years, so he knows how life is to be lived. He's the counselor, which makes him OK. Since Mrs. Fangschleister is coming for help, obviously she's Not OK. It all works out wondrously. She is presenting herself as Victim-with-a-Problem. He can play the role of Rescuer-with-the-Answer. The scene starts with some apparently Adult-Adult information going back and forth. She loads it with "secret messages" that invite Reverend B. to play Parent to her Helpless Child. He's willing; indeed, he's been waiting all day for a Victim to drop in.

Through tears, whiny voice, little-girl body language, and Cons like "I'm helpless," she invites him to the Game. He accepts through his fatherly voice and other indications that he's there for her to lean on. Her invitations are the Con, his acceptance the Handle. The "counseling session" proceeds as the invitations and acceptances are exchanged, masked all the while by Adult-Adult discussion of The Problem. The invitations and acceptances grow stronger until she is ready to spring her trap—to throw the Switch and collect the Payoffs.

"Reverend Bodelschwing, do you really think you can help me?" What a Con! How can he possibly know whether or not he can help? But he *wants* to be helpful, so he says, "Yes, Mrs. Fangschleister. Together we will solve your problem." He has taken the bait. He is solidly hooked.

Now for the Switch. She moves from Helpless Child to Critical Parent, and she *bombs* his Child. "What makes you preachers think you can solve every problem that comes along?" She gets up and leaves, immensely enjoying her threat never to return to his church again. Reverend B. feels like a discarded Eskimo Pie wrapper. (This is a *true* story!)

This was a mutual Game in that both Kids got what they wanted. She can feel bad because "even the church" couldn't help her. She "bared her soul" to the pastor for nothing. He was a "know-it-all" like the rest. She'll just have to go home and keep on doing whatever she was doing before. But in the process she put the reverend in his place. The reverend, too, was collecting Stamps. "See what happens when you do Jesus' work! You get crucified. Move over, Jesus. Make room for me."

Both get a reinforcement of their picture of how life "has to be," precluding any possibility of change. Meanwhile, they stroke each other; they say "I see you." Even after the Game, each can continue to find strokes as they review the operation. "You tried to find help, Emma. It's those preachers who are the problem." And: "You tried to help her, Wolfgang. If she knew half as much as you do, she wouldn't be messed up in the first place." Stroke, stroke!

In the funnies, Dagwood is getting his usual sandbagging from Blondie in a Game. After dinner Blondie asks Dagwood, "How was your dinner, dear?" He, mistaking her question as a request for strokes, responds, "Gee, it was perfect." Now for the Con. "Oh, come on, Dagwood. Nothing is perfect" (Hook, Hook, Hook). From among the dozens of options open to him, Dagwood chooses to compromise. "Well, then . . .let's just say it was *almost* perfect." Now the Switch. "I knew you'd find something wrong with it!" NIGYYSOB! She's proved her "point" once more, and he's feeling his usual, incompetent, "where-did-I-go-wrong" self.

Playing a Game is like going around the block to get next door. A Game precludes any possibility of living in the here-and-now, which is the only place life can be lived.

We were singing "Holy, Holy, Holy" a couple of Sundays ago. I had always taken the line "Though the eye of sinful man thy Glory may not see" to be a Parental decision. "You were a bad boy, and so God won't let you take a peek at him."

Not so. "Sinful man"—the guy who stands on his own udder playing Games instead of living life—cannot be in touch with the glory of God or the glory of Life.

I stopped at a traffic signal. On the bumper of the car ahead was a sticker, "In case of Rapture this car will be unmanned." "Rapture" is interpreted by certain fundamentalists as the time when Jesus will come again and all the White Hats (the people who go to *their* church) will dissolve into thin air and experience "The Rapture." Their motto seems to be "Never drive or fly with a real Christian because the Rapture might come." The rest of us "hated-by-God" folk will be left to fend for ourselves.

I have no way of knowing what was going on in the head of the guy with the bumper sticker, but it occurred to me that the words have a hostile content. "My Soul Is Better Than Your Soul" is an adaptation of the basic Game "Mine Is Better Than Yours." I don't think Jesus died on the cross so this guy could put ha-ha signs on his car. *Spiritual* games of "Mine Is Better Than Yours" aren't any more useful than *secular* ones.

In his book *One Inch from the Fence,* Wes Seeliger talks about the Protection Racket some churches enjoy playing.* Coming from the Persecutor role in the Game triangle, they find people to Victimize. "God hates you! You will roast in hell! Good news! You are eternally damned!" When they find people willing to play Victim, they throw the Switch, move to the Rescuer role, and "save" the person they've just beaten into submission. As Wes points out, it's not unlike Al Capone and his boys "protecting" the store they plan to destroy.

Other churches figure they'll give people the Word more quickly if they come on as Rescuers from the beginning. They search for causes to espouse, anything and everything. If they persist in "trying to help" long enough, sooner or later someone will kick them. Now the Victims of this unwonted persecution, they collect the Stamps due them for "trying to be like Jesus."

---

*If you haven't read Wes's book, run (do not walk) to the nearest bookstore and buy a copy. You'll laugh a lot while reading it *and* pick up a lot of new insights.

Still other churches begin their operation from the position of the Victim. They emulate what they think Jesus did: They wear hair shirts, do a lot of fasting, suffer all the time. These people can make a cross out of two Coke bottles. They love to quote the passage from Isaiah that speaks of "the suffering servant." But when the time is right, they can move to either the Rescuer or Persecutor role to entrap the other person.

The Gaminess of these three forms of church life lies in the ulterior transactions involved. While professing to spread the Good News, these churches are preoccupied with a hundred other things—like winning the "Who has the most sheep?" contest.

Good News can be spread only a very straight sort of way. "Hey, guys. Wanna hear something that turns me on?" If they say "No!" it's time to move on. There are lots of folk around who *are* looking for what you have to say. Every man has a right to stay miserable if he wants to—maybe he's happy being miserable—and maybe he isn't as miserable as we think. Jesus said not to give pearls to pigs (see Matthew 7:6). A pig isn't bad. Pigs just don't want, don't need, don't know what to do with a necklace.

Converting a guy against his will with Games is no conversion at all, and basically it's un-Christian. If we can't do it straight, we can't do it, period. All the turkey suppers and spaghetti dinners and hay rides and songfests in the world aren't going to trick people into living the faith. Besides, I think it's blasphemous to decide that the gospel can't stand on its own feet.

Henry Hitt Crane, a Methodist preacher who was in Detroit at the time, told us seminarians a great story. He had taken a fishing trip with his father up on Pike's Peak. As they approached a favorite lake in their horse-drawn buggy, they found a strange character dressed in robes and a turban. Obviously he was "guarding" something. He thrust his lance across the road.

"Halt! Whither goest thou?" the strange one asked.

"Well, " said Crane's father, "we're planning to go fishing in the lake."

"Dost thou mean harm to yon sacred mountain?"

"No. We just want to fish a little."

The man looked them over for a minute and then said, "Pass!"

As they rode along, Crane's father said, "Henry, do you understand what we just saw? That damned fool is protecting a *mountain*!"

If God is truly God, he doesn't need our protection anymore than the mountain needed that nut's sentry duty. If God's message is worth hearing, people will hear it. Convoluted and Gamey attempts to "make it heard" will only get in his way!

12

Unless You Become
As Little Children

You have a clever, determined, unbending four- or five-year-old inside you. The Child ego state can single-handedly withstand both the other ego states. To test this, ask a smoker what each of his ego states thinks of this activity. I always get something like:

> PARENT: It's disgraceful for a grown man not to be able to control himself.
> ADULT: There is strong evidence that smoking can be harmful to your health.
> CHILD: I don't care what you guys say, I'm gonna smoke!

This determination evidences itself in many other areas of life, too. The Kid finds ways to do what he thinks he has to get done, and he does it in spite of opposition from both Parent and Adult.

A woman won't quit crying. Her Adult knows crying won't help, and her Parent scolds her for it. But her Kid keeps on crying. You scream at your wife even though both your Parent and your Adult are opposed to the idea. Your Child "knows" what he "has to do"! You have work to do but your Child stares into the middle distance and gathers wool, and no matter how hard your Adult and Parent push, you don't get started.

I want you to understand that your Child ego state has power of incredible proportions. The Child contains all your tapes about survival issues, including the urge to live and the desire to somehow make it in this world of giants. He will somehow find his daily requirement of fuzzies and pricklies even though he's seldom allowed to get them in straight fashion. Without permission to pay attention to himself, he plays Games, collects Trading Stamps from his Rackets, and uses any and all situations for his own purposes.

In most of us the poor Kid has to do all this by himself while carrying his Critical Parent on his back. The Child has another burden. As we saw in Chapter 6, most of us have our Child locked up in a suitcase inside an asbestos-lined trunk stashed down in the basement. We were told our Child is not only "childish" but also dangerous. He's full of "unconscious" urges and primal forces that can kill, so we lock the little bastard up before he gets us in trouble. The result: The Kid turns guerrilla fighter. He sleeps by day and travels by night, blending into the foliage, stealing pies off the back windowsill of strange houses, and striking his "adversaries" as best he can.

It doesn't have to be that way! Once you understand and believe the motto "The Child always wins," you are free to use your Adult and Nurturing Parent to help the Kid win and win *well* instead of using your Critical Parent to knock him unconscious for another week.

People have trouble understanding that the Child always wins, but it's true inside your head and it's true between biological parents and their offspring, too. When mama "made you go to church," you had three options, and whichever you chose, you won!

> 1. You went and decided to have a good time and learn something for yourself.
>
> 2. You complied but you pouted, stared at the ceiling, heard nothing, and sent a hundred "I hate you" messages to mama (which "ruined" her Sunday). Your Child got what *he* wanted.
>
> 3. You refused to go. You rebelled.

In both 2 and 3 your Child collected some Trading Stamps. In all three he got stroked. The Child always gets what he thinks he needs. A friend of mine used to be put in a closet when she was "a bad girl." "Go stand in the closet for ten minutes," they would tell her. Know what her Kid did? She'd stay in the closet for four hours after her time was up. Used to drive her folks crazy. Kids are powerful.

A young man came to us for group therapy. He wanted to "get on with his life." He wasn't keeping a job or staying in college. He didn't relate to girls well. He was thirty, but he was still living in his childhood home. He wanted to change these things.

Although a number of "problems" were involved, the key was the fantastic stubbornness of his Child. He reported, "I can't think of anything to say to a girl." Not even a fantasy. His "couldn't" was a "wouldn't," since there are thousands of things to say. Some of them don't mean much, granted. But this guy's Kid wouldn't say *anything*. When asked to remember events from a few years back, he "couldn't." When asked about his homework assignment, he announced he had failed to get around to it. The therapist noticed that a small grin would appear with each "couldn't," and with each report of failure, some piece of this client thought it was all pretty cute. One night he complained that he lacked awareness. "Do you know any technique that will make me more aware of what's going on?" The answer was no, because his secret message was, "Try to make me aware and I'll show you how stubborn a guy can be!"

As he began to get in touch with how beautifully stubborn he was—as he began to enjoy openly his ability to resist anyone anywhere and anytime—and as he got in touch with how useful his stubbornness had been to him as a child, he decided to use his stubbornness more selectively. He would be stubborn when it helped, but not otherwise. From that point on therapy was a breeze. Within two months he had a new show on the road. He had reached his goal for coming to the group and he liked it.

The point is, you *will* go where your Child leads you, but

you'll do it more effectively and more happily when you *like* the little guy and know what he wants and needs. If he's hungry, feed him. If he's tired, let him rest a tad. If he needs attention, get some for him. Your Adult can protect you from the things you fear, like "laziness" or "greed," by setting appropriate time limits and quotas.

If your Kid wants excitement, for example, find something exciting and sensible and let him do it. People who don't have permission to get excited will find their excitement in a crooked fashion. Many couples fight with each other as a way of finding excitement. In therapy it takes them a while to discover they aren't fighting about *serious* issues. Fighting is a good way to let yourself know you're alive and to keep the juices flowing, but there are *better* ways.

For years I've said, "When you work in weather and religion, you have to make your own excitement." Ever watch the TV weatherman when a tropical storm appears? You'd think he was reporting the fall of the Kremlin. His voice deepens and crackles. "Tropical storm Delilah is now only three thousand miles away and traveling straight for us at three miles an hour!" I should imagine weathermen are grateful for tropical storms, since they break the monotony.

In churches folk who are not yet in touch with the real excitement of living expectant lives "with God" have to make their own excitement. Like going to the barricades to fight against installing an electric organ instead of a *pipe* organ. Like fighting over doctrinal issues that even when solved, don't change anything. New mission churches are always great places for bored people; being financially shaky, they constantly "skate on the brink of disaster." Getting the buildings up and equipment together provides unthreatening activity. All this can be fun for Kids who need excitement. When the church gets larger, people frequently report that "something is missing of late."

To be worth living (for Kids, at least) life must be exciting. People who shy away from really exciting things manufacture their own "safe" excitement. "That ball almost hit you in the eye!" mother screams. Now that the danger is past, she's still

finding excitement: "What if it had put your eye out? What if
. . . What if . . ." What-ifs are nice, safe, manufactured
excitements. One way I can get excited is by deciding to feel
rushed. "Oh, I've only got five minutes and there's *so much* to
do!" "So much" consists of running a comb through my hair,
checking the back door, and picking up my briefcase. Elapsed
time, forty-eight seconds.

The Child can cause trouble if ignored, but more im-
portantly, he is the only part of us that can *experience* life.
The Parent is a stored collection of yesterdays, and the Adult
processes data in a disinterested way—so the Child is the only
part of us that can say "Wow!" I think "Wow!" is the key
word in abundant life. A motto: Life is great in direct
proportion to the number of times you say "Wow!"

We theologians have used the word "holy" a lot. To me,
"holy" always meant something better than me, far off and
unreachable. I understood the idea, but it never helped me
much. These days I see "holy" differently. "Holy" is a *real,
everyday encounter with life that allows me to say "Wow!"*
Remember Moses' encounter with God in the burning bush?
Alone atop a mountain, he experienced life "bigger than life."
The Bible reports God saying to Moses, "Take off your shoes,
Mosheh. You're having a holy experience. You're standing on
holy ground." I think when our Child runs into the holy,
burning bushes of life, our sandals fall off *automatically!*
Unless we've glued them on!

A new insight comes and changes my life for the better.
Wow! The pale-green fuzziness of the fir tree in my backyard
pitched against a not-usual-for-Houston blue-blue sky. *Wow!*
Somebody's artistic talents sweep me to new heights. *Wow!* A
love relationship transports me into new, unexplored depths
within myself. *Wow!* I wake up and discover I'm getting to live
for another whole day. *Wow!*

There are a lot of wows around, because there are lots of
places where the ultimate touches the present. But only the
Child will see or hear them. Only the Child can feel and experience the holy—the now—the wow.

Consider for a moment what your three ego states would do

if confronted with a "burning bush" experience. Your Adult would figure out the BTU rating. Your Parent would caution you not to get too close. But your Child would be filled with wonder.

Lots of folk still want a formula that guarantees admission to heaven, and maybe a "reserved seat" besides. If that's all they want, I advise them to stuff a carrot in their left ear. That makes as much sense as the handy-dandy formulas I hear being passed out.

Whatever else salvation is, either theologically or psychologically, it is being in the *now* and saying *wow*. It's being all in one piece. Or as Paul said, "I have learned to be content in whatever situation I find myself" (Philippians 4:11).

Jesus said that unless we become as little children, we won't be able to enter the kingdom of God. Parent-types have always translated this to mean, "If you don't obey me and submit to what I tell you to do, if you aren't compliant and timid and if you don't shut up when I say 'Shut up,' I won't let you go to the Big Ice Cream Party in the Sky." If your Parent wants to believe that, okay, but I don't think it's true, accurate, or helpful.

In the first place, as any biological parent will tell you, children aren't at all like any of the things I just said. They don't obey, they aren't timid, and they seldom shut up just because someone says to. I think Jesus understood children and had something quite different from the Parental view in mind.

So what's a *little* kid got that most of us have trouble getting? I can think of a couple of things. Little kids are autonomous. They may be dependent on others for food, clothing, and the like, but they control their own insides! Since they haven't begun adapting to the expectations of others, they do what *they* want to do *when* they want to. If they feel scared, they run, or cry, or scream, and without wondering what they "should" do. If they're happy, they giggle without deciding whether or not it's proper.

Little children possess awareness. Kids see things that

adults pass over. They haven't yet developed "cognitive processes," so they don't spend much time thinking *about* things; they simply experience them. They are aware of the world outside them, and they are aware of the world inside them. Little children spend very little time remembering the past or programing the future. A fight between two three-year-olds lasts only two minutes, and they're back playing together again.

Grown-ups have learned to generalize. When I go to a rummage sale, I report I saw "a lot of junk." Little ones, on the other hand, see all 200 items. They see colors and shapes and textures. They see the tiniest picture on a porcelain plate. My "intelligence" keeps me from seeing a lot of my world.

I'm not opposed to thinking—it serves us well—but we can spend more time "in our heads" than we need to. To the degree we are "in there digging around," we are not using our senses to discover the world around us. Little children are aware.

Kids are also candid. Don't ask a little fellow a question if you don't want a frank answer. "Mamma, who's that big, fat lady?" Sammy asks in his usual 75-decibel voice that's heard three floors up. Mamma gets the cold sweats. Sammy doesn't mean to be offensive; it's just that she's really fat! Tell the kid to eat his pickled okra and he reports, "It tastes like *worms!*" (I agree.) Preadaptation children are honest!

Kids also live in the here-and-now. Ask a kid whether he'd rather have a nickel now or a dollar tomorrow and he'll take the nickel, because for him there's no tomorrow. As we grow older we learn it's useful to plan ahead, and the habit takes over until we are spending most of our time living in tomorrow—that is, when we're not living in the past. Consequently, we miss what's going on right now. A kid never does. He's bright-eyed and bushy-tailed about life.

Finally, kids are spontaneous. Because they are autonomous, aware, candid, and living in the here-and-now, they react spontaneously to what's going on around them. When the stimulus quits, *they* quit also.

All of these traits of little children make the parent nervous.

(Perhaps you heard your Parent picking at some of the paragraphs above.) Parent ego states scare easily. They think of a million "what ifs" and *plan* for them. Spontaneous Kids can ruin Parental plans, but they serve you very well by finding the intimacy, joy, and reality of life.

When Jesus performed miracles, the disciples were amazed. If you want to see miracles today, your Child must see them, for Parents don't get amazed. They say, "Well, it was about time this happened!" Or, "I've seen better shows in my day." Adults simply record the event. The Child says "Ho boy!"

Whatever else we may know, we know that the power and glory are in our Child. That's where the action is. Grown-ups tend to be scared of Kids. A "prominent businessman" wonders, "If I let my Kid out, he might ruin me." He decides to lock him up. His Kid proceeds to ruin him in devious ways—like making life tasteless, or sad, or tense and horrible. Like millions of Frogs before him, the businessman dies wondering, "What the hell was *that* all about?"

There's more to life than merely pleasing the Child in us. There's a need for social responsibility, and TA does not help us discover the definition of that dimension of life. It does not deal with concepts of love, sacrifice, justice, or mercy. It doesn't explore creation—or purpose. It never speaks of "God."

But the emphasis that TA places on the value of the Child is essential to these other areas. Social responsibility will not be explored, let alone accepted as something of concern, by people with beat-up, undernourished Child ego states. When they *are* examined by people with hurting Kids, the "exploration" is always Gamey.

Sammy joins the church "to help establish justice," but his Kid is starved for strokes. All his efforts to "straighten out the world" will be Gamey attempts at finding strokes and bad feelings until his Child has what *he* needs. Then Sam can effectively work for change. He will quit scolding and faultfinding. He will sacrifice himself only when the sacrifice effects change. He will nurture those around him—enemies as well as friends—instead of being a toxic person-with-a-cause. Because *he* is full, he will be able to fill others. (A Kid with a mote in his eye can't really help others see more.) Someone else said, "We love because he first loved us."

Give your Kid a break. Feed him. He's not a monster. He's a neat Kid! Like all Kids, he needs a Parent to nurture him and an Adult to take care of him. Given these helpers, he becomes the power and the glory within us.

13

You Are *You*, So Rejoice!

The one single point I want you to hear in this chapter is, to find the abundant life, you "must" understand the faith statement, "Because you exist, you matter." People stay in trouble because they don't believe they matter. Most people emerge from infancy with a sense of guilt, imposed by the surrounding society. "Why should I be here?" What few warm fuzzies they have received have been for "good behavior." They figure they get what they need only when they perform, and since this "works," they conclude they don't matter *unless* they perform and perform well.

The problem of Sammy Fangschleister is Justifying My Existence. "Why should I be alive? Who would want me? How could I possibly be OK?" The Rich Young Ruler's question is being echoed by millions. "What must I do to be saved, to matter?" It is the question of all Adapted Children. The matter of self-justification implies that we are Not OK. Looking for the power and the glory, we find grief instead. Torn apart by the expectations of everyone around us, we seldom live our own lives. To get what we need (purpose, attention, strokes) we try Games and Rackets and crooked transactions, which further alienate us from God, others, and ourselves.

When Jesus hit the Palestinian scene two thousand years

ago, he encountered a world full of religious NIGYYSOBers—Critical Parent Pharisees who beat on the Adapted Child temple-goers with their "religious wisdom." Poor Schlomo Fangschleisterstein had 613 rules and regulations to fulfill each day—just to stay even! Most days he probably broke from five to fifty of them. No wonder he felt Not OK. His spiritual adviser helped him—"to try harder."

To these poor folk Jesus proclaimed the good news that God loved them just as they were. He showed people a way to feel good about who they were. He gave them new permission to turn down their unproductive Parent tapes: "You have heard it said of old . . . but I say unto you . . ." He showed folk how to use their Adult in making religious value decisions: "The Sabbath is made for man, not the other way around." His potent Parent opened doors. "He spoke as one having authority."

They should have let him stay around. When people are saved, they become autonomous people. They live their lives aware of what's going on around them and inside them. They see themselves as OK Children of God. They start making their own decisions, living their own lives. In living out the fullness and freedom of this salvation, their joy and zest begin slopping over onto the people around them. "My cup runneth over!" This enables other people to feed on freedom and find "salvation."

But society's Parent tapes can't abide autonomous people. Society and Parents want to control, not save people. It didn't take many centuries for the church to abandon Jesus' picture of a loving Father and replace it with a Critical Parent image. The banner "God loves you" was pulled down, and "God'll get you!" was hoisted in its place.

Jesus preached justification by *faith*. When you ask, "How are we justified?" whatever answer you pick, you're acting on *faith*, not *proof*. Christ said we are justified by our faith that we are individual creations of God, that we matter simply because we *are*.

Parents are usually terrified of this kind of theology. It might give people the bighead. "If they start thinking they're OK just as they are, no telling what kind of rape and murder and plunder their bigheads will lead them to do!" That Parent tape doesn't make any sense. No one ever went berserk because he liked himself. People go crazy, act crazy, or think crazy because they don't like themselves. When I *feel* alienated from God, others, and myself, I will *act* alienated and thus *become* alienated in fact.

Jesus said it doesn't have to be this way. We don't have to *find* justification for ourselves—we *are* justified. God forgives us while we sin. That kind of forgiveness can heal a man. I don't have to *become* whole, I simply need to experience my wholeness.

This is a crucial point: We already have within us what we need for health. We already know what we need to do to move forward. We have been taught, however, that we need to look outside ourselves. Orthodox Christianity declares that Jesus was wrong: "The Kingdom of Heaven is *not* within us! Someone else holds the key. Go looking." So we take endless classes, go through hundreds of different rituals, and move from guru to guru, hoping we will somehow become more clever, more potent, more aware. After all, didn't Jesus say some people were Not OK?

No! Jesus obviously didn't like some of the things people did. His anger waxed when one man's actions harmed another man's life. He took a whip to the folk in the temple who were turning religion into a farce. He confronted the ways men kept themselves stuck and invited others to join them, calling "stuck" religion.

But Jesus never equated Not-OK acts with Not-OK people. To say, "Because *I* don't like what you do, you are a Not-OK person," is to discount the other person. Jesus never assumed that the Pharisees were evil, or stupid, or morally handicapped. Although he frequently didn't like what they said or did, he took them seriously as OK people. He saw them as people who were struggling with life and coming up with answers that were harmful to others and to themselves. To the end of his life he saw them as OK. "Father, forgive them, for they don't know what they're doing."

Some scholars are asking what they call the "ontological question": "Who says we're so OK?" I would raise a prior question: Who says we're not? Who says we must constantly be justifying our right to exist?

The Pharisees, the prostitutes, the thieves, the merchants in the temple were justified people, but because they didn't *know* it, they spent their lives trying to justify themselves—the prostitute with her body, the Pharisee with his rules and regulations.

Parent-types don't like many of the things Jesus said, but he said them! What to do about that? The answer that "religious" Parents have found down through the years is to make "faith" synonymous with "works." The RSPV (Revised Standard Parent Version) became, "You will be justified when your faith measures up to the authorized standards, and I'll tell you what those standards are."

What irony. Jesus proclaims grace—a free gift. He says we can live in the wow-now of God's world. But others have altered the free gift to make it one that must be earned. So, many people say, "God loves me just as I am," without believing a word of it. What they really think is, "God accepts *me*? Well, yes, *if* I shape up to some standard that somebody has concocted."

I'm convinced Jesus wanted us to be potent and change the world. When a person knows he's *OK* even though he does things "wrong," even though he's a sinner, his faith gives him a potency that changes the world. "Ask and you'll get it; seek and you'll find it; knock and it'll open to you" (see Matthew 7:7). People who think they're Not OK don't believe this either, and find sneaky (sinful) ways to get what they really need. Winners ask, seek, knock.

Jesus met a centurion whose servant was seriously ill. This Roman military leader knew that Jesus was potent and could cure his servant. Whenever the centurion himself ordered things, they happened. He sensed that Jesus could do the same thing, and he said so. Jesus was astounded. "*Nowhere* in all of Israel have I seen such faith," he said (see Matthew 8:5 ff.). Faith is a potent operation.

The person who latches onto a faith that declares "I matter because I exist" is free for the first time to take charge of his life. Declaring that others matter simply because they exist allows him to live in an OK-OK position.

The myth that God hates us and will stomp us the first time he catches us screwing up has turned the Christian gospel into a string of flypaper. Instead of becoming "saved," we feel more damned. Like the savage who worshiped the weather but couldn't do anything about it, we spend our lives trying to please God and failing. The more we fail, the more we sin (the more entrapped we become).

We fail because we listen to Parent-created mustought-should myths—myths that hinder instead of helping. Let me use a story to help me define "myth." A three-year-old girl wanted her mother to produce her a baby sister. The mother tried to explain that this took time. The little girl countered that they could pick one up at the Safe-Way store.

"Why do you think we can get one there?"

"Because every time I'm at the Safe-Way, I see the ladies with babies in their baskets." The kid's observation had grown to become a myth.

Many of our myths are perpetuated by songs and sayings. How about "You *made* me love you; I didn't *want* to do it, I didn't *want* to do it." Holy cow! Sounds like a bum way to start relating. Or, "You always hurt the one you love." I once had a guy in group who honestly believed this was true. It had been true in his childhood home. Mom and dad (who must have loved each other, right?) were constantly hurting each other. Shaped by their example, he had gone to innumerable women "looking for love" (meaning, hurting them and being hurt by them). If he spent two hurtless days with a woman, he was "losing her love."

Parent tapes and Child crazies are full of myths that aren't useful: "When confused, don't disturb people by asking for the information you need." "Don't tell people where you are." "Life is a vale of tears." "You don't have a right to feel what you feel." "Good people always suffer." Hogwash!

Jesus said that if your hand, or foot, or eye is your undoing, get rid of it. Better to enter "heaven" maimed or blind than to hang onto all your parts and go straight to hell (see Matthew 5:29-30).

If Jesus was for throwing away arms and legs that "undo" us—like one full of gangrene—he certainly would be for getting rid of the mustoughtshoulds that kill. Like the myth that declares, "I am a wretch and there is no wholeness in me." Cut! Or, "If it's pleasurable, it's also immoral." Out! What a damnable lie.

I have a friend who says, "Who's cuter than God?" She *likes* God. She doesn't mean he can't be a serious God, for he deals with grim things like life and death and pain and sickness and the rest. But he's also fun to live with, and she likes to be around him. If God can be all things, he can be fun too! But Parents feel that God mustoughtshould be solemn and serious. He has to be a drag in order to be eligible for such a high position in the church.

I used this illustration in a worship service and a hundred eyebrows went up. I think the alarm comes from our Protestant Work Ethic. We have been brainwashed into believing there is a split between work and play. Work is productive and good; fun accomplishes nothing and is often evil. Medicine that tastes good doesn't work.

Remember Jesus' parable about the guy who worked himself to death growing things and then building barns to store the things in? "You dope," says the parable. "Don't you know you're going to die tonight? Who will the things belong to then? What will you have gotten out of life?" If you have a Parent tape saying that if you're enjoying yourself you aren't accomplishing anything, throw it into the fire!

Another myth: People report that being in a group involves a "threat" or "risk" or "tension." They report a fear of "exposure." A Martian would have trouble *seeing* the risk involved in two people talking to each other. The "risk" is in their head. How does it get there? In almost every case, I have discovered a Parent tape that says something like, "When someone asks you a question or makes a statement to you, you have to answer and you have to tell the truth!"

With these myths in our heads we find a world of "risk" around us. Let's say someone asks at a cocktail party (probably because he's drunk!), "How many people have you been sexually intimate with?" Our blood runs cold, our nerve endings start to jangle,and cold sweat emerges. We wish we had stayed home and worked a crossword puzzle instead of "risking a relationship." But this question is threatening only to an Adapted Child who must get everything right, and get it right by answering truthfully. We have a lot of options to such a question. We can simply remain silent and smile. We can say, "None of your business." We can ask, "Why do you want to know?" We can be cute and say, "I know but I'm not going to tell you." Or we can decide we don't care to be close to a person who seems so aggressive. Each response is potent and effective. The boor who asks such dumb questions will succeed in "threatening you" only if you let him.

Another myth holds that busyness is the same as "pressure." "I'm under such pressure!" we say when playing "Harried and Bothered." The pressure is in our head. I gave a trainee permission (he had ordained me to give him permissions, or it wouldn't have worked) to take off from work on a busy day, as an experiment. He took the day off and enjoyed himself, although the "pressure" stayed with him. His Parent wouldn't shut up. In the process, though, he learned how to turn down the tape. And on his return to work (much refreshed), he discovered that the sky hadn't fallen because of his absence. He learned that since the "pressure" was in his head, he could control it.

A lot of us suffer from the myth that we cannot accept our total experience unless it *all* clicks. "I love my husband, *but* he drives me crazy." "But" is a blot on human experience. "But" means "Ignore what I just said."

"You preach well, Reverend, but you leave me confused." Cancel! "You have a lot of friends, Sammy, but some of them don't seem very genuine." Blooey! "I'm working hard but I don't amount to much." Crash! "But" discounts, forbidding me the joy of the first part of a sentence.

The woman above *does* love her husband; she *also* has some trouble with him. Both are valid parts of her human experience. In TA we train people to use the word "and" whenever it applies, which is most of the time. Try it. As we learn to accept all of our experience, we get more in touch with ourselves and with our world. At first people think we're being picky-picky by paying attention to such words, but in time they find the discrimination helps them to be potent.

Being impotent is tough. (I'm not talking about our plumbing, although it's tough there, too.) Being impotent means being ineffective, helpless. I feel impotent when I come up behind a truck that says "Danger! Radioactive!" What am I supposed to do? Lag behind? Drive past it? Pray? That's impotence. Impotence is watching your wife roll down the hall into the operating room. It's hearing an avalanche above you. It's reading that the Middle East crisis is widening. Situations like these force impotence on us; most of life's situations, however, do *not* require us to be impotent. We can usually be potent *if* we have the permission.

Potency makes for winning. Being potent means getting done what you set out to do. It means understanding your potential as well as your limitations. It means feeling good about yourself.

This book is running out, and before it does, I'd like to give you some starter suggestions for acquiring potency. They come from real-life folk who have shed their Frog skins and now dance in God's sunlight.

Take responsibility for your own life. When Adam decided to "eat the fruit," he got caught. Like most little boys, he grabbed for an alibi. He told God, "The woman *you gave me*—she gave me the fruit!" This is the first recorded invitation to play "If It Weren't for You."

If you're feeling tense, be aware that you are tensing yourself. If you're feeling depressed, pay attention to how you are pushing yourself down. One of the most useful questions for anyone who's learning to be response-able is: "How am I deciding to feel scared (lonely, depressed, angry)? How am I deciding to be impotent?"

When you hear your answer, don't scold yourself for the "dumb way you've been acting." You won't ever explore yourself if it's going to get you scolded. I always know when one of the people I'm working with is headed to "health." He comes breathlessly into the group and says, "Wow, I've found out something else I've been doing that's not helping me." Instead of feeling guilty, ashamed, or depressed, he's happy. The new information brings joy.

Stop scolding and fussing. Scolding and fussing perpetuate the problem. Options never occur to people while they're fussing.

Feel what you are feeling. Get in touch with your own feelings. Don't scold yourself for being crabby if you're really feeling crabby. It's hard to be effective or potent when you pretend.

Give yourself warm fuzzies. Use your Nurturing Parent to give yourself the strokes you need. If no one else will tell you what a good job you did, tell yourself. And believe yourself. It's a darned poor Parent who can't think of something nice to say to his own, hurtin' Child.

As you begin taking *all* the warm fuzzies others offer (if only a smile on the street) *and* giving yourself still more, you'll notice that cold pricklies quit feeling cold and prickly. With your stroke basket full, you'll quit snatching at negative strokes. If you're going to duck strokes, duck the nasty ones!

Learn to ride the bus facing forward. Morris and Natalie

Haimowitz of Chicago point out that many people "ride the bus backward." People know where they've been but don't know where they are. When these folk come to group, they talk about what they were feeling in group the week before. I have a friend who never gets excited while on a trip; he only gets excited when he's home and *talking about* his trip. I'd rather be excited *while* I'm doing something exciting.

Turn off the auto-pilot when trouble starts. We do most of the things we do rather automatically and perfunctorily. From habit. From practice. Anita Plummer says we work as though we have an "auto-pilot"—a little black box into which we program what we're supposed to do under certain conditions, for instance, "Fly seven miles east and turn forty-five degrees north."

We put these auto-pilot instructions in our heads a long time ago. At the time, they may have been useful—and they may still be. But if they aren't useful, we need to "hand-fly" the airplane until we "get around the mountain." When we find a solution, we can reprogram the auto-pilot and switch it back on.

At first it's scary to fly the plane manually after so many years on auto-pilot. With practice, however, you gain a sense of potency from flying the thing yourself.

Insist on clarity. Adapted Children are supposed to *guess.* People with Parents on their backs are supposed to fill in the blanks and "get it right." Unique Children of God can insist on clarity.

Clarity is a two-way street. I insist on hearing clearly what you want me to hear; I want you to hear me clearly. In either case, the *speaker* is responsible for being clear.

Most of us figure that "too much clarity" can get us into trouble. If you don't believe that, watch what happens in a restaurant when the three-year-old announces, "Got to poo-poo." The parents immediately instruct him in the "adult" talent of obfuscation! Some folk don't want to hear clearly. We also learn to build in some ambiguity. We speak fuzzily so that later we can say, "No, that's *not* what I meant!" and get away with it. Lack of clarity may sometimes be useful, but it's *not* very potent.

The Child's clarity is a tool for potency. "Mary, I'm tired and I want to leave this party in ten minutes" is a clear and understandable message. But "Mary, I'm worried about the baby-sitter. Do you think she is old enough to be working so late?" is not clear unless you really intend to discuss the baby-sitter's age and the propriety of her working late. A marital Game of "Uproar" can develop when Mary chooses to defend the baby-sitter's abilities. The husband, growing more tired by the minute, finally shouts, "Mary, I will not leave that girl alone for another second!" (Mary can now wonder if she's losing her husband to a fourteen-year-old.)

Being clear means sending *single* messages. Jesus said, "Let your eye be single." Nobody can look two places at once, and no one can *successfully* say two things at once. If you're complaining to your son about his bad grades, don't smile, else your son's Child will see the smile and decide you like for him to goof off.

People never know what to do with the "double whammy" of an unclear message. A double whammy is a father yelling through the bathroom door at his son, "Whatever you're doing in there, quit it!"

You have a right to hear other people clearly. When someone says, "Why are church people such phonies?" you have a right to know what it is they want you to hear. There are alternatives:

    a. You're a "church people" and I don't like *you*.

    b. I want to tell you about my last disastrous experience with church people.

    c. I would like to discuss the relative correlation of religion and straightforwardness, philosophically speaking.

    d. Please notice my disappointment over what has happened to me.

    e. I dare you to make me go to church again.

Pay attention to how unclearly you and your friends speak. I am amazed that we ever communicate.

In your home is this kind of question asked?

> HUSBAND: Is breakfast ready yet? (Meaning: *I'm late for work and I'm hungry and I want to be fed right now!*)
> WIFE: I'm working as fast as I can considering I have to get three children ready for school! (Meaning: *If you'd put the bread in the toaster, we would get to eat a lot sooner.*)

Speaking in code retards communication. The same holds true for "in-head" conversations. Feeling depressed, I decided to make a list of things I didn't like about my life. First item: "I'm growing older."

What's "growing older?" As I examined that phrase, I realized how unclear it was. Why be depressed about growing older? It beats hell out of the alternative. Also, my first thirty years of "growing older," I *liked.* For the next fifteen, I didn't think about it. So, why am I now upset over "growing old?"

I got down to the things that were *really* bothering me: "I'm not lying on the floor and listening to records anymore. I'm not playing with the kids as much as I'd like. My activities are much too routine." And so on. None of the things I disliked was a function of growing older. I could change any or all of them if I wanted. Believing my unclear "growing older" meant feeling helpless; instead, I found some things I *could* do.

We keep ourselves confused if we aren't clear (in concrete terms) about what we tell ourselves.

"Don't push the river; it flows by itself." This is Fritz Perls' great motto. The quickest way to feel impotent is to try to push a river. Lots of things can stand a little pushing—wheelbarrows, bicycles, carts full of watermelons, paint brushes, lawn mowers. But rivers don't need pushing. They have their own flow, their own inertia. Pushing only messes up things like kids going through puberty, creative thoughts,

feelings, motivation, sleeping dogs, kids going through public school, stubborn Child ego states.

Pushing helps *when* someone *asks* for a push; otherwise, it seldom does. If my car is stuck in the mud and I ask for a push, the push is gratefully accepted. If I'm peddling my bike as fast as I can and you run up and push me:

a. It makes me nervous.
b. It makes my feet move too fast.
c. When they move too fast and hit something, they break!
d. In any event, I *resent you*!

I don't think Fritz Perls was just being poetic; I think his analogy is apt. "Pushing a river" accomplishes nothing except to tire out the pusher. Parent ego states love to push. "No one will move if you don't push them," daddy-in-the-head says. The truth is: Damn, damn the pusher man!

St. Paul said: "Don't be overpowered by evil; use good to overpower evil." I think that's a pretty heavy message for people who like to think they are "powerless." The translation reads: "You don't have to lie down and let bad things walk over you. You are as potent as they are; more potent, often. Take charge! Take the good things you understand and use them to wipe out the things that make life insufferable for you."

Becoming potent is deciding to be what you were created to be, to do what needs doing, to take charge of your own life. It's a neat way to live. Some folk are already living that way. You can too if you wanna. Wow!

Postlude

A postscript, but I prefer the liturgical expression. This is the song I sing as I conclude this worship of mine. And, besides, I don't want to be "scripty," right?

My TA/Christian primer is done. I've shared with you some things I've learned and experienced. Ideas, insights, and feelings from within myself and from other people. Only one more thing to share.

Some early-time Israelis heard Jesus speak, were captivated by the possibilities of his message, and wanted more for themselves. They asked, "Teacher, where are you staying?" They probably wanted to know about his motel.

Instead of telling them his address, he invited them, "Come and see." He wasn't talking about a place. His invitation was to "come live with me." Just *hearing* a message, or even thinking about it, doesn't cut it. Having learned something, our next step is to apply it, live it. Those who found abundant life with Jesus were those who walked with him, who ate the dust of the road with him, who drank wine and broke bread with him.

Good idea! "Come and see." If you've run into some helpful ideas, don't lose them in your head. See for yourself if they work. Use the ideas. Your life is as valid as the next person's.

Postlude

And they were bringing children to him, that he might touch them; and the disciples rebuked them. But when Jesus saw it he was indignant, and said to them, "Let the children come to me, do not hinder them; for to such belongs the kingdom of God. Truly, I say to you, whoever does not receive the kingdom of God like a child shall not enter it!" And he took them in his arms and blessed them, laying his hands upon them.

Mark 10:13-16

Bibliography

Berne, Eric. *Games People Play.* New York: Grove Press, 1964. A detailed explanation of game analysis; not for laymen or popular reading.
————. *Sex in Human Loving.* New York: Simon and Schuster, 1970. A fun book. Excellent look at relationships.
————. *Transactional Analysis in Psychotherapy.* New York: Grove Press, 1961. Berne's unpacking of his new theory for the psychiatric community. It uses mostly Freudian terms, is scholarly and tedious reading. For scholars only. Incidentally, the theory has changed considerably since this book.
————. *What Do You Say After You Say Hello?* New York: Grove Press, 1972. Berne's last book, a treatise primarily on life scripts. Easy to read; many new ideas, some of which did not catch on. Potpourri of both TA and Freudian "leftovers." For advanced reading.
Birnbaum, Jack. *Cry Anger.* Don Mills, Ontario: General Publishing Co., Ltd., 1973. A good look at TA with the emphasis on anger. Only book to do that so far.
Harris, Thomas A. *I'm OK—You're OK.* New York: Harper & Row, 1967. The book that popularized TA. A primer, yet not all that easy to read. Academic.
James, Muriel, and Jongeward, Dorothy. *Born to Win.* Reading, Mass.: Addison-Wesley, 1971. A fine unpacking of TA theory, with Gestalt exercises at the end of each chapter to help the reader get more in touch with himself.
Meininger, Jut. *Success Through Transactional Analysis.* New York: Grosset and Dunlap, 1973. An excellent book. Many everyday examples of how TA can be applied. My first choice for people I work with.
Steiner, Claude M. *Games Alcoholics Play.* New York: Grove Press, 1972. An analysis of life scripts. Well worth reading.
————. *Scripts People Live.* New York: Grove Press, 1974.
Schiff, Jacqui. *All My Children.* New York: Pyramid, 1970. A novel-like, easy-to-read description of her work with schizophrenia. Exciting!

Bibliography

GESTALT BOOKS

Perls, Frederick S. *Gestalt Therapy Verbatim.* Moab, Utah: Real People Press, 1969. Fritz at work. Good reading.

————. *In and Out the Garbage Pail.* Moab, Utah: Real People Press, 1969. Perls' rambling through his thoughts. Not for the easily shocked, but fun and serious.

Stevens, Barry. *Don't Push the River.* Moab, Utah: Real People Press, 1970. Gestalt, people, and theology from a woman's point of view.

THEOLOGY

Oden, Thomas C. *Game Free.* New York: Harper & Row, 1974. Best work on intimacy I've read. Good use of TA but inaccurate criticism of it.

Seeliger, Wes. *One Inch from the Fence.* Atlanta: Forum House, 1973. WOW!

PUBLICATIONS

Back copies of both the *Transactional Analysis Journal* and the *Transactional Analysis Bulletin* may be ordered from Transactional Publications, 1772 Vallejo Street, San Francisco, California 94123.